In This Issue

PIVOT MAGAZINE

Founder
Jason Miller

President
Juddene Villarin

Web Master
Joel Phillips

Designs
ReliableStaffSolutions.com

Copyright © 2025 PIVOT

ISBN: 978-1-957217-90-1

Contact

Jason Miller
Founder
1151 Eagle Drive #345
Loveland, CO 80537
jason@strategicadvisorboard.com

Shelby Jo Long
Editor-in-Chief
shelby@strategicadvisorboard.com
877-944-0944

From the Editor

Growth Is Not Guesswork

This month, we're getting practical.

In an era where every click, scroll, and purchase is trackable, growth is no longer just about big ideas. It is about using the right strategies, tools, and insights to scale smartly. The May issue of Pivot was built for business leaders who are ready to move from inspiration to execution.

You will find strategies for acquiring clients without overspending, creating loyal communities through customer-centric marketing, and using analytics to make smarter decisions. We are not talking about fluff. We are talking about the kind of actionable guidance that separates momentum from noise.

Growth is a formula. It is a mindset. And it is entirely within reach.

Wherever you are in your journey, this issue is designed to give you the clarity and tools to take the next step with intention. Let us build something that lasts.

Shelby Jo Long
Editor-in-Chief

From the Desk
Of The President

Scaling with Precision and Purpose

This issue is about scaling the right way.

We know that real growth does not come from throwing money at the problem. It comes from asking better questions, tracking what matters, and staying relentlessly focused on your customer.

In this issue, we spotlight the strategies that work. How to attract the right clients. How to retain them. How to turn data into direction. And how to grow your business without losing control of your time, energy, or resources.

What makes this issue powerful is not the complexity. It is the clarity.

So here is the challenge I will leave with you:

- What are you measuring that actually drives growth?

- How do your marketing strategies reflect the people you serve?

- Where can you grow more by spending less?

Let us scale smarter. Let us lead with focus. Let us keep building businesses that are both agile and unshakable.

JUDDENE VILLARIN *J.V.*

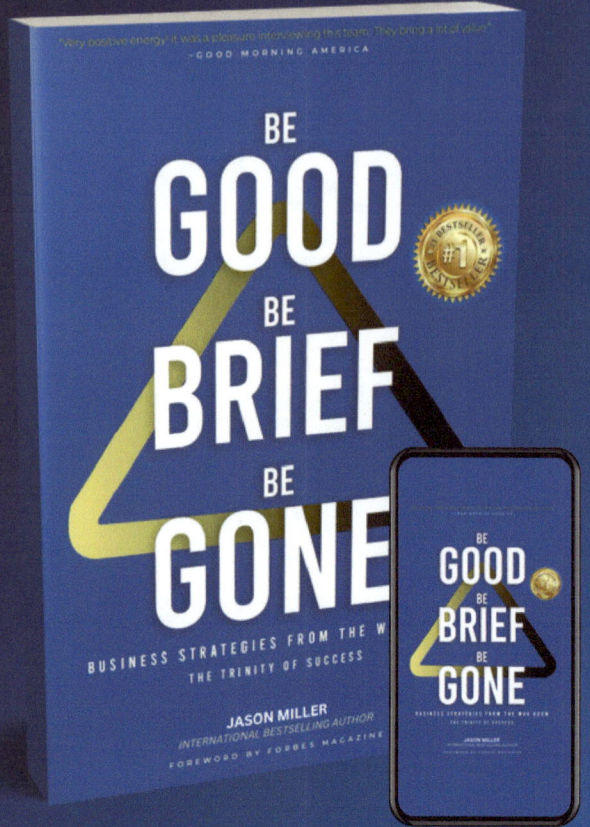

Clocked Out: Why the 40-Hour Workweek Is Dead

The Lie We've Lived

The 40-hour workweek is a relic. It is a museum piece we continue to worship. While we stream content at lightning speed, summon groceries to our doorstep, and run companies from couches, we still chain ourselves to a system designed for factory floors and timecards. And we call it normal. We are told to work hard, climb the ladder, and maybe someday we will deserve rest. But what if the ladder is leaning against a crumbling wall? What if the hustle is just another trap?

Entrepreneurs, founders, and leaders are waking up. Not all at once, not everywhere, but the tide is shifting. The question is no longer whether the 40-hour workweek should survive. The question is why it is still clinging to life.

The Origin Story No One Questions

Let's get one thing straight. The 40-hour workweek was never built for the knowledge economy. It was forged in the early 20th century when laborers fought tooth and nail for basic rights. Henry Ford implemented the 40-hour schedule not out of generosity but to increase productivity and reduce turnover. It was revolutionary in its time, but that time is long gone.

Today's work is not measured in widgets. We do not stop being productive when we leave a factory gate. Ideas do not clock out. Innovation does not follow a punch card. Yet somehow, the 40-hour structure has remained the default blueprint, even for startups and digital-first companies.

The Global Shift That Proves the Point

Let's look beyond our borders. Iceland ran one of the largest trials of a reduced workweek between 2015 and 2019. Workers moved to a 35- or 36-hour schedule without a drop in pay. Productivity remained the same or improved. Stress levels dropped. Well-being soared. Eventually, 86 percent of Iceland's workforce gained the right to shorter hours.

In the UK, a six-month pilot of the four-day workweek in 2022 included over 60 companies.

The result? Fifty-six decided to keep it. Revenue held steady or grew. Employees reported less burnout and higher satisfaction. A simple change unlocked massive impact.

Microsoft Japan experimented with a four-day workweek and saw productivity jump by 40 percent. That is not a typo. Forty percent.

These are not isolated miracles. They are data points in a pattern too bold to ignore.

Why So Many Leaders Still Resist

So if the results are this obvious, why do so many corporate leaders double down on the old ways? The answer is simple. Control. Legacy thinking. Fear.

The 40-hour model is familiar. It is a known quantity. Leaders who grew up equating work ethic with long hours feel threatened by change. Some still believe productivity looks like people at desks from nine to five. Others simply do not trust their teams. There is also the myth of hustle culture. That toxic whisper that says if you are not grinding 24/7, you are falling behind. But the truth is, overwork is not a badge of honor. It is a slow-motion burnout.

Entrepreneurs at the Crossroads

For founders and small business owners, the tension is even sharper. On one hand, the dream of flexibility and purpose drove them to start something. On the other, survival in a brutal market pushes them into overdrive.

The trap is this: many entrepreneurs escape corporate life only to recreate its worst parts in their own ventures. They hustle harder, sacrifice more, and then wonder why they feel empty.

But there is a shift underway. Smart founders are building businesses that reject the old rules. They are designing teams for outcomes, not hours. They are trading burnout for longevity.

Take Steph Smith, a remote-first entrepreneur who built a content business around asynchronous work. Or Basecamp's founders, who famously embraced calm productivity and banned long hours. Or startups like Wildbit and Buffer, which publicly share their four-day policies and productivity gains.

These leaders are not lazy. They are strategic. They understand that rest is not the opposite of work. It is a force multiplier.

Gen Z Isn't Asking for Permission

And then there's Gen Z. The most connected, skeptical, and values-driven generation to enter the workforce. They watched their parents burn out. They saw the cracks in the corporate dream. And they are not here to play pretend.

Gen Z workers are questioning everything. Why commute if you can be just as effective from home? Why work 40 hours if 32 gets the job done? Why tie self-worth to a paycheck when purpose matters more?

They are not lazy. They are focused. They are allergic to waste and performative work. And they are forcing businesses to adapt or fall behind.

Remote Work Cracked the Illusion

The pandemic did not invent this conversation. It simply broke the spell. Once millions of people experienced remote work, the illusion shattered. The office was never about productivity. It was about proximity. About control.

Remote work proved what many already suspected. Most meetings are unnecessary. Most managers micromanage because they are insecure. Most of the day is not productive time, just performative presence.

When the illusion broke, something powerful happened. Workers started asking better questions. And companies had to start giving better answers.

Capitalism, Rewritten in Real Time

This is not just a workplace issue. It is a capitalism issue. The old model is built on extraction. More hours, more output, more profit. But that model is collapsing under its own weight.

Investors are no longer just chasing short-term gains. They are looking at ESG. They are asking how businesses treat people, not just margins. Customers are voting with wallets. Workers are walking away from toxic jobs. The system is being rewritten.

Capitalism is not going away. But it is being forced to evolve. And that means rethinking how we define value. Not in hours logged, but in impact created.

The Data Does Not Lie

Study after study confirms it. The majority of knowledge workers are productive for only three to five hours per day. The rest is filler. Distraction. Pretend work.

Companies that adopt flexible or reduced-hour models see gains in retention, morale, and even revenue. A 2023 Gallup report found that employee engagement spikes when workers have autonomy over their time.

And burnout? It is not just a vibe. It is a business risk. The World Health Organization classifies it as an occupational phenomenon. And the cost of burnout in lost productivity and turnover is measured in billions.

Founder Stories That Break the Mold

Meet Ali. She runs a design studio with a global team. Her rule is simple. Four-day weeks, no after-hours Slack, and sabbaticals after major projects. Her company grew 30 percent last year.

Or Rahul, who runs a consulting agency. He gives his team Fridays off every second week. He says they hit deadlines faster and clients are happier.

Or Yuki, a Tokyo-based entrepreneur who cut her team's hours by 25 percent but doubled down on strategic planning. The result? Less churn, more innovation.

These are not unicorn stories. They are examples of what happens when leaders value outcomes over optics.

The Myths That Must Die

Myth one. People will slack off if you reduce hours. Reality? Slackers slack off in any system. The right people rise to the challenge.

Myth two. Clients expect round-the-clock service. Reality? Clients expect results, not martyrdom.

Myth three. We cannot afford to reduce hours. Reality? You cannot afford burnout, turnover, and disengagement.
Myth four. Hard work means long hours. Reality? Smart work means sustainable success.

What Comes Next

This is not a trend. It is a transformation. The businesses that survive the next decade will be the ones that adapt. Those who cling to the past will be left behind.

The 40-hour week is dead. It just has not been buried yet. What takes its place is not one perfect model. It is a mindset. A willingness to design work around life, not the other way around.

Flexible hours. Async collaboration. Remote-first teams. Outcome-based performance. These are not perks. They are survival strategies.

A Call to Action

If you are an entrepreneur, founder, or business leader, you are not just running a company. You are shaping culture. You are writing the future of work in real time.

Ask yourself. What kind of workplace are you building? What kind of life are you making possible? Are you replicating a broken model, or are you brave enough to build a better one?

Work is changing. The market is changing. People are changing. You can fight it, or you can lead it.

The 40-hour workweek is dead. Let it go. And in its place, build something worth waking up for.

The Rise of Social Commerce: What Businesses Need to Know

Social commerce has become more than a passing trend. It represents a fundamental change in how people discover, evaluate, and purchase products. By blending social interaction with shopping, it has created a new kind of marketplace that operates inside the platforms where people already spend much of their time.

At its core, social commerce is the buying and selling of products and services directly through social media platforms. This has blurred the traditional lines between browsing for entertainment and making purchases. What once required multiple steps across different websites can now happen within a single app.

Commerce has evolved into a dynamic experience where discovery, inspiration, and purchase often occur in the same moment. Consumers can watch a video, read a review, and complete a transaction without ever leaving their social feed.

Platforms like Instagram, Facebook, TikTok, and Pinterest have become far more than social networking sites. They are now bustling marketplaces where brands, influencers, and consumers interact directly. The path from interest to purchase has never been shorter or more seamless.

Businesses that recognize and embrace this change are tapping into vast and engaged audiences.

They are not only selling products but also building communities and fostering lasting customer relationships through content and conversation.

On the other hand, companies that hesitate to adapt risk losing relevance. Consumers expect brands to meet them where they are, and today that means within their favorite social apps.

This article explores the rise of social commerce, how it has evolved, the impact it has on traditional retail, the major platforms driving growth, user engagement strategies, common challenges, and what the future holds for businesses aiming to thrive in this new environment.

Historical Perspective: From Social Interaction to Social Transaction

The journey of social commerce began subtly. In the early 2000s, platforms like **MySpace** and later **Facebook** became the first social networks where users shared product recommendations and reviews. This informal word-of-mouth marketing became the foundation for what would evolve into structured social commerce.

Early Milestones:

- **2005-2008:** Facebook introduced business pages, enabling brands to interact directly with consumers.

- **2010:** Pinterest launched, giving users a visual bookmarking tool that organically drove product discovery.

- **2013:** Instagram started allowing ads, beginning the transformation into a commerce platform.

- **2016-2018:** Facebook introduced Marketplace and Instagram added "Shop Now" buttons, blending social and shopping experiences.

This evolution was fueled by one simple observation: People trust people. Unlike traditional advertising, social media fostered peer-to-peer trust and authentic recommendations.

Current Trends and Market Size

Social commerce today is a multi-billion dollar industry experiencing explosive growth.

Key Statistics:

- According to Statista, global social commerce sales reached **$1.3 trillion** in 2023 and are projected to surpass **$2.9 trillion by 2026**.

- In the U.S., **35% of social media users** have made at least one purchase directly through a social platform.

- Gen Z and Millennials are leading the charge, with **60% of Gen Z consumers** using social media to discover products.

The COVID-19 pandemic accelerated this trend, as lockdowns pushed both consumers and businesses to embrace online platforms for daily needs and shopping.

Why Social Commerce Works

At the core of social commerce's success are **three psychological drivers:**

1. Social Proof: Seeing others purchase or recommend a product builds trust.

2. Frictionless Experience: Integrated shopping tools reduce steps from discovery to purchase.

3. Personalization: AI and algorithms curate product suggestions based on user behavior and preferences.

Major Platforms Powering Social Commerce

1. Instagram

- **Instagram Shops** allow brands to create storefronts.

- Integration with **Meta Pay** enables seamless checkout.

- **Reels Shopping** turns video content into direct sales opportunities.

2. Facebook

- **Marketplace** serves as a peer-to-peer and brand-consumer sales platform.

- **Facebook Shops** integrate with Shopify, WooCommerce, and BigCommerce.

3. TikTok

- **TikTok Shop** integrates in-video shopping experiences.

- Viral challenges often spark mass purchases (e.g., #TikTokMadeMeBuyIt phenomenon).

4. Pinterest

- **Shopping Pins** and visual search help users discover and buy products intuitively.

5. WhatsApp and Messenger

- **Conversational commerce:** Businesses sell directly through chat apps with integrated payment options.

Key Features and Benefits for Businesses

- **Personalized Recommendations:** AI-driven suggestions tailored to individual users.

- **Seamless Transactions:** In-app checkout reduces drop-off rates.

- **Community Building:** Brands foster loyalty through interactive content and social engagement.

- **User-Generated Content (UGC):** Authentic customer photos and reviews act as persuasive marketing.

User Engagement Strategies

Businesses succeeding in social commerce adopt advanced engagement strategies:

- **Influencer Marketing:** Partnering with micro and macro influencers to tap into niche audiences.

- **Interactive Content:** Quizzes, polls, AR filters, and shoppable live streams.

- **Exclusive Offers:** Time-limited discounts or early access to products for social followers.

- **Loyalty Programs:** Rewarding repeat purchases and encouraging sharing.

Challenges and Solutions

Challenge	Solution
Data Privacy & Security	Invest in secure payment gateways, transparent data policies.
Platform Dependency	Diversify sales channels. Maintain an independent e-commerce presence.
Content Management	Implement content moderation tools and encourage authentic reviews.
Customer Service	Deploy AI-powered chatbots and omnichannel support strategies.
Changing Algorithms	Stay agile. Continuously test content formats and ad strategies.

While social commerce offers immense opportunities for growth and customer engagement, it also presents a range of challenges that businesses must proactively address. Ensuring data privacy and security is essential to maintaining customer trust, while reducing platform dependency protects against sudden changes in policies or algorithms. Effective content management safeguards brand integrity by promoting authenticity and relevance. To meet evolving customer expectations, businesses can enhance service with AI-powered chatbots and streamlined omnichannel support. Adapting to changing algorithms requires agility and a commitment to continuous experimentation with content and advertising strategies. By embracing these solutions, businesses can navigate the complexities of social commerce and position themselves for long-term success.

Impact on Traditional Commerce

Traditional retailers can no longer afford to view social commerce as optional.

Brick-and-Mortar Integration:

- QR codes linking to online shops.

- In-store social walls featuring UGC.

- Buy Online, Pick Up In Store (BOPIS) strategies integrated with social campaigns.

Case Example:

Sephora bridges online and offline by integrating AR makeup trials on Instagram with in-store experiences.

Real-Life Success Stories

1. Glossier

Built a billion-dollar brand by turning everyday customers into brand advocates through Instagram and community-driven content.

2. Gymshark

Leveraged influencers and UGC to become a leading fitness apparel brand, with a direct-to-consumer model heavily reliant on social commerce.

3. MVMT Watches

Scaled from a small startup to a major watch brand through Facebook and Instagram ads, influencer collaborations, and community engagement.

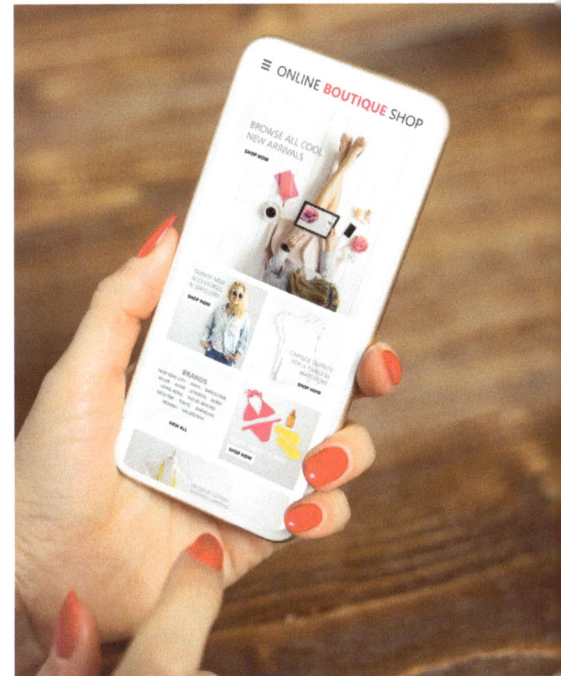

Future of Social Commerce

Emerging Technologies:

- Augmented Reality (AR): Virtual try-ons for fashion and beauty.

- Virtual Reality (VR): Immersive, shoppable virtual stores.

- Blockchain: Transparent payment systems and NFT-based loyalty programs.

- AI: Hyper-personalized recommendations and predictive analytics.

Consumer Behavior Shifts

One of the most significant forces shaping the future of commerce is the ongoing shift in consumer behavior. As digital experiences become more integrated into daily life, the way people discover, evaluate, and purchase products is evolving rapidly.

Social-first Shopping has emerged as a dominant trend. Today's consumers are not just using social media to connect with friends or follow brands. They are actively discovering new products, exploring reviews, and making purchases directly within their favorite social apps.

Platforms like Instagram, Facebook, TikTok, and Pinterest have become not only sources of entertainment and inspiration but also critical points in the purchasing journey. This shift has blurred the lines between social interaction and shopping, creating a seamless experience where discovery and conversion happen almost simultaneously.

Values-based Buying is also influencing a growing portion of consumer decisions. Shoppers are no longer focused solely on price or convenience. They are increasingly making choices that align with their personal values, such as sustainability, ethical sourcing, and social responsibility. Brands that demonstrate a genuine commitment to environmental stewardship, fair labor practices, and community engagement are finding stronger connections with consumers who seek to support businesses that reflect their beliefs. Transparency and authenticity are no longer optional but expected, and companies that fall short may quickly lose favor.

Community Commerce is reshaping how people shop together and influence each other's purchasing decisions. Group buying models, which offer discounts or benefits when multiple customers purchase together, are growing in popularity. Additionally, peer-to-peer selling and the rise of micro-entrepreneurs on social platforms have empowered individuals to become both consumers and sellers. Online communities, niche groups, and influencer-driven marketplaces have created dynamic ecosystems where commerce is driven by relationships, recommendations, and shared interests.

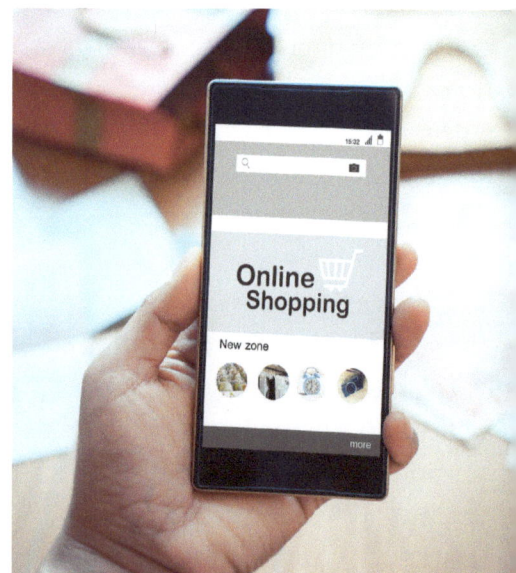

Spotlight on Strategy:

Paula Abanes

Creative Pulse Behind the Screens

"Working at RSS has taught me the incredible power of leveraging digital platforms to make tangible business impact, no matter where you're located"

STAFF STATS

🎧 Work Anthem: Stronger by Kanye West

🍪 Favorite Snack: Chicken wings

💡 Fun Fact: I cook the best sisig and adobo (according to my fiance ●)

When did you join the RSS team, and what brought you here?

I joined the RSS team in 2023. I saw a fantastic chance to use my skills to help companies thrive.

What's your favorite part of working at RSS?

I love the trust and autonomy, especially remotely, and seeing the direct impact of managing a client's social presence.

How has your role evolved since you started?

I began with content execution, now lead strategy, analytics, and course creation for diabetes. Deeply meaningful due to my family's experience.

Describe your typical workday or work-from-home setup

My day blends content creation, visuals, data analysis, and team collaboration—all from my home office, starting with client channel check-ins.

If you could describe RSS in three words, what would they be?

Supportive, empowering, and resourceful

Reliable is about delivering high-quality work on time, anticipating needs, and being someone both my client and RSS can count on, especially in a remote working environment.

These behavioral shifts underscore the importance of understanding not just what consumers buy, but how and why they make purchasing decisions. Brands that can anticipate and respond to these changes will be well positioned to capture attention, build loyalty, and thrive in a constantly evolving digital marketplace.

Strategic Takeaways for Businesses

1. **Prioritize Authenticity:** Build trust through transparent and value-driven content.

2. **Invest in Technology:** Utilize AI, AR, and data analytics to enhance user experience.

3. **Diversify Channels:** Don't rely solely on one platform.

4. **Leverage UGC and Influencers:** Harness the power of community to amplify reach.

5. **Stay Agile:** Social media trends and algorithms change rapidly. Test, learn, and adapt.

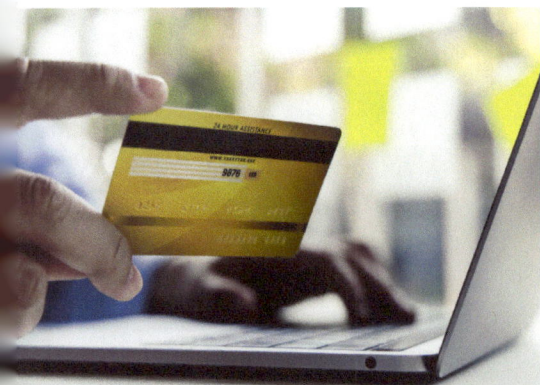

Social commerce is not a passing trend. It represents the future of retail and a fundamental shift in how consumers interact with brands and make purchasing decisions. The blending of social interaction and shopping has created a new landscape where connection fuels commerce and commerce, in turn, strengthens connection.

This new reality offers businesses an unprecedented opportunity. Those that recognize the synergy between community engagement and sales will be better positioned to meet the evolving expectations of digital consumers. Adaptability and responsiveness are no longer optional but essential for long-term success.

Brands that fail to embrace this change risk being left behind. The marketplace is increasingly defined not just by the products sold but by how, where, and through whom those products are discovered and purchased. Consumers expect seamless experiences that align with their habits, preferences, and values.

As the boundaries between community and commerce continue to dissolve, businesses must move beyond simple transactions. The focus should shift toward building authentic relationships, fostering trust, and delivering value beyond the point of sale.

The most successful brands will be those that create memorable shopping experiences, engage meaningfully with their audience, and position themselves as both providers of products and active participants in their customers' lives. Social commerce is not just an evolution of retail. It is a transformation that will shape the future of how people connect, shop, and engage with brands.

Innovative Marketing Strategies to Reach Your Target Audience

Marketing has always been the engine that drives businesses forward. Whether a company is just starting out or is an established brand, the ability to attract, engage, and retain customers is essential for growth and success. In recent years, however, the marketing landscape has undergone a remarkable transformation. Advances in technology, changes in consumer behavior, and the rise of digital platforms have created both challenges and opportunities for marketers.

Gone are the days when traditional advertising methods like print ads, billboards, and television commercials were enough to capture attention. Today's consumers are more informed, more selective, and more empowered than ever before. They expect personalized experiences, valuable content, and meaningful engagement from the brands they choose to support. This shift has made it necessary for businesses to

explore innovative marketing strategies that can break through the noise and resonate with their target audience.

This article will explore a wide range of innovative marketing strategies. From understanding your audience to leveraging the power of content marketing, influencer partnerships, social media engagement, and email campaigns, we will provide actionable insights and practical

tips to help businesses connect with their audience in meaningful ways. Whether you are a small business owner, a startup founder, or a seasoned marketing professional, this guide will equip you with the knowledge you need to succeed.

Understanding Your Target Audience

Before implementing any marketing strategy, it is essential

to develop a deep understanding of your target audience. This step forms the foundation of any successful marketing effort. Knowing who your customers are, what they value, and how they make purchasing decisions allows you to tailor your messages and campaigns for maximum impact.

Start by gathering demographic information. Age, gender, location, income level, education, and family status are all valuable data points. This information helps you create customer profiles or personas that represent different segments of your audience.

Beyond demographics, delve into psychographic information. Understand your audience's interests, hobbies, values, beliefs, and pain points. What motivates them to buy? What challenges do they face? What solutions are they seeking? By answering these questions, you can create marketing messages that speak directly to their needs and desires.

Analyzing buying habits is equally important. Learn how your audience makes purchasing decisions. Do they rely on online reviews? Are they influenced by social media recommendations? Do they prefer to shop in-store or online? Knowing their behavior helps you choose the right channels and tactics for reaching them.

There are several tools and methods for gathering this information. Conduct surveys, host focus groups, and analyze website analytics. Social media platforms also provide valuable insights into audience behavior and preferences. Additionally, customer relationship management (CRM) systems can help you track and segment your audience for more personalized marketing.

Content Marketing: Building Trust and Authority

Content marketing has emerged as one of the most effective ways to connect with an audience. Rather than pushing products or services directly, content marketing focuses on providing valuable information that educates, entertains, or inspires.

Start by identifying the types of content that resonate with your audience. Blog posts, articles, videos, podcasts, infographics, and social media posts are all popular formats. Choose the ones that align with your brand and audience preferences.

Consistency is key. Develop an editorial calendar to plan and schedule content regularly. This helps maintain a steady presence and keeps your audience engaged.

Quality is equally important. Your content should be well-researched, well-written, and professionally produced. It should provide genuine value and address your audience's needs and interests.

Search engine optimization (SEO) is another crucial element. Optimize your content with relevant keywords, meta descriptions, and internal links to improve visibility in search engine results. This increases the likelihood that your content will reach a wider audience.

Storytelling is a powerful technique in content marketing. Share stories about your brand, customers, and community. Stories create emotional connections and make your content more relatable and memorable.

Finally, encourage interaction. Invite your audience to comment, share, and engage with your content. This not only boosts visibility but also fosters a sense of community and loyalty.

Influencer Marketing: Leveraging Trust and Reach

Influencer marketing has gained significant traction in recent years. By partnering with individuals who have established credibility and a loyal following, brands can tap into new audiences and build trust.

The first step is identifying the right influencers. Look for individuals whose audience aligns with your target market. Consider not only the size of their following but also the level of engagement and the values they represent.

Micro-influencers, those with smaller but highly engaged audiences, can be especially effective. They often have more personal relationships with their followers and can drive higher conversion rates.

Once you have identified potential influencers, focus on building genuine relationships. Engage with their content, provide value, and approach collaborations with mutual benefit in mind. Authentic partnerships are more likely to resonate with audiences than purely transactional ones.

When creating influencer campaigns, prioritize transparency.

Ensure that sponsored content is clearly disclosed, as this builds trust with the audience. Work with influencers to develop content that feels natural and aligns with both their style and your brand message.

Track and measure the success of influencer campaigns using metrics such as reach, engagement, website traffic, and sales. This allows you to assess the return on investment and refine your strategy over time.

Social Media Marketing: Creating Conversations and Community

Social media has revolutionized the way businesses interact with

Platforms like Facebook, Instagram, Twitter, LinkedIn, and TikTok offer unparalleled opportunities for engagement and brand building.

Start by choosing the right platforms based on where your target audience spends their time. Not all platforms will be relevant for every business, so focus your efforts where they will have the greatest impact.

Develop a content strategy that includes a mix of promotional, educational, and entertaining content. Use high-quality visuals, compelling captions, and clear calls to action.

Engage with your audience regularly. Respond to comments, answer questions, and participate in conversations. This shows that you value your audience and fosters a sense of community.

Paid advertising on social media can also be highly effective. Use targeted ads to reach specific demographics, interests, and behaviors. Experiment with different ad formats, such as carousel ads, video ads, and story ads, to see what resonates best.

Leverage features like live streaming, stories, and polls to create interactive experiences. These features not only boost engagement but also provide valuable insights into audience preferences.

Monitor your social media performance using analytics tools. Track metrics such as reach, engagement, click-through rates, and conversions to evaluate the success of your campaigns and make data-driven decisions.

Email Marketing: A Direct and Personal Connection

Email marketing remains one of the most powerful tools for connecting with your audience. Despite the rise of social media and other communication channels, email offers a direct and personal line of communication that few other methods can match.

Building a targeted email list is the foundation of any successful email marketing campaign. Start by encouraging website visitors to subscribe to your newsletter. Offer incentives such as discounts, exclusive content, or free resources to encourage sign-ups. Make sure your sign-up forms are easy to find and user-friendly.

Once you have built your list, focus on creating engaging content. Your emails should provide value to your subscribers, whether through educational content, product updates, special offers, or personalized recommendations. Use a friendly and conversational tone to create a sense of connection.

Segmenting your email list allows you to send more relevant messages to different groups within your audience. For example, new subscribers might receive a welcome series, while loyal customers

might receive exclusive promotions. Segmentation increases the relevance of your messages and improves engagement rates.

Personalization is another key to successful email marketing. Use your subscribers' names, recommend products based on past purchases, and tailor content to their interests. Personalized emails tend to have higher open and click-through rates.

Finally, measure the success of your campaigns. Track metrics such as open rates, click-through rates, conversions, and unsubscribe rates. Use this data to refine your strategy and continually improve your email marketing efforts.

Personalization: Making Every Interaction Count

Personalization has become a cornerstone of effective marketing. Consumers expect brands to understand their needs and preferences and to deliver experiences that feel tailored to them.

Start by collecting data about your customers. This can include demographic information, purchase history, browsing behavior, and interactions with your brand. Use this data to create detailed customer profiles.

Personalization can take many forms. On your website, recommend products based on a visitor's browsing history or past purchases. In your email campaigns, tailor content and offers to individual preferences. On social media, engage with users based on their interests and previous interactions.

Dynamic content is a powerful personalization tool. This technology allows you to display different content to different users based on their data. For example, a first-time visitor to your website might see a welcome message and an introductory offer, while a returning customer might see personalized product recommendations.

Behavioral triggers can also enhance personalization. Send follow-up emails to customers who abandon their shopping carts or offer special discounts to those who have not made a purchase in a while.

The goal of personalization is to make every interaction feel meaningful and relevant. By showing your customers that you understand and value them, you can build stronger relationships and drive loyalty.

Emerging Technologies: Staying Ahead of the Curve

Technology continues to reshape the marketing landscape, offering new tools and opportunities for innovation. Staying informed about emerging technologies can give your business a competitive edge.

Artificial intelligence (AI) is transforming how marketers analyze data, predict behavior, and automate tasks. AI-powered tools can help you segment your audience, personalize content, and optimize your marketing campaigns.

Chatbots and virtual assistants are becoming increasingly popular for customer service and engagement. These tools can handle common inquiries, guide users through the purchasing process, and provide support around the clock.

Augmented reality (AR) and virtual reality (VR) are enhancing the customer experience by allowing users to visualize products in their environment or experience virtual events. These technologies can be particularly effective in industries such as fashion, home decor, and real estate.

Voice search is another growing trend. As more consumers use voice-activated devices, optimizing your content for voice search can improve visibility and accessibility.

Blockchain technology is also making its way into marketing, offering new possibilities for secure transactions, transparent supply chains, and innovative loyalty programs.

By embracing emerging technologies, you can create more engaging, efficient, and personalized marketing experiences for your audience.

Experiential Marketing: Creating Memorable Moments

Experiential marketing focuses on creating memorable experiences that engage consumers and leave a lasting impression. This strategy goes beyond traditional advertising by immersing the audience in a brand-related event or activity.

Events, pop-up shops, workshops, and product demonstrations are all examples of experiential marketing. These experiences allow consumers to interact with your brand in a tangible and meaningful way.

Interactive digital experiences can also be a form of experiential marketing. Virtual events, webinars, and interactive content like quizzes and games can engage audiences and foster a sense of participation.

Storytelling is a key component of experiential marketing. By weaving your brand's story into the experience, you create a deeper emotional connection with your audience.

Experiential marketing can generate significant word-of-mouth promotion. Attendees often share their experiences on social media, extending the reach and impact of your campaign.

To be effective, experiential marketing should be aligned with your brand values and resonate with your target audience. Planning and execution are critical to ensuring that the experience is positive and memorable.

Partnerships and Collaborations: Expanding Your Reach

Partnerships and collaborations can be powerful strategies for expanding your reach and connecting with new audiences. By joining forces with other businesses, influencers, or organizations, you can leverage each other's strengths and resources.

Look for partners that share your values and target a similar audience. Collaborations can take many forms, including co-branded products, joint events, cross-promotions, and content partnerships.

Collaborating with complementary businesses can provide mutual benefits. For example, a fitness apparel brand might partner with a health food

company to offer bundled promotions or co-host wellness events.

Nonprofit partnerships can also enhance your brand image and connect you with socially conscious consumers. Supporting a cause that aligns with your values can foster goodwill and strengthen customer loyalty.

Effective partnerships require clear communication, defined goals, and mutual respect. Establishing roles, responsibilities, and expectations upfront can help ensure a successful collaboration.

Customer Experience: Building Loyalty and Advocacy

The customer experience encompasses every interaction a consumer has with your brand. Providing a positive and consistent experience is essential for building loyalty and turning customers into advocates.

Start by ensuring that your products or services meet or exceed expectations. Quality and reliability are fundamental to customer satisfaction.

Communication is another key aspect. Keep customers informed throughout their journey, from initial inquiry to post-purchase support. Be responsive to questions and feedback.

Personalization can enhance the customer experience. Tailor communications, offers, and support to individual preferences and needs.

Convenience is also important. Simplify the purchasing process, offer flexible payment options, and provide easy access to support.

Encourage customer feedback and use it to improve your offerings and processes. Showing that you value and act on feedback builds trust and demonstrates a commitment to continuous improvement.

A positive customer experience can lead to repeat business, referrals, and positive reviews, all of which contribute to the growth and success of your brand.

Data Analytics: Informing and Refining Your Strategy

Data analytics plays a crucial role in modern marketing. By collecting and analyzing data, you can gain valuable insights into your audience's behavior, preferences, and responses to your marketing efforts.

Start by defining clear objectives and key performance indicators (KPIs) for your campaigns. This allows you to measure success and identify areas for improvement.

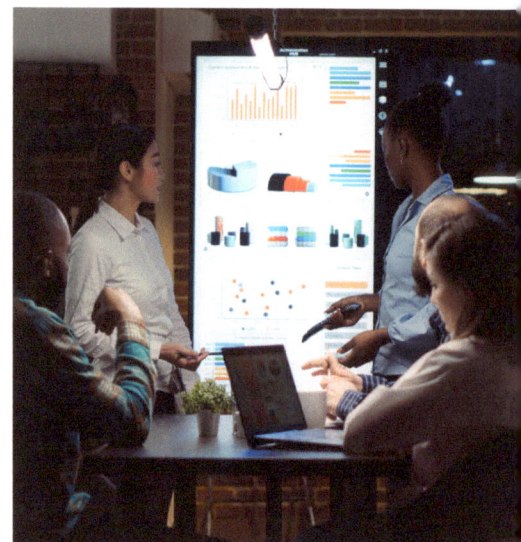

Use tools such as Google Analytics, social media insights, and CRM systems to track metrics like website traffic, conversion rates, engagement levels, and customer lifetime value.

Analyze patterns and trends to understand what is working and what is not. Use this information to refine your strategies and make data-driven decisions.

Predictive analytics can also be valuable. By analyzing historical data, you can anticipate future trends and behaviors, allowing you to proactively adjust your marketing efforts.

Data privacy and security should always be a priority. Ensure that you comply with relevant regulations and handle customer data responsibly.

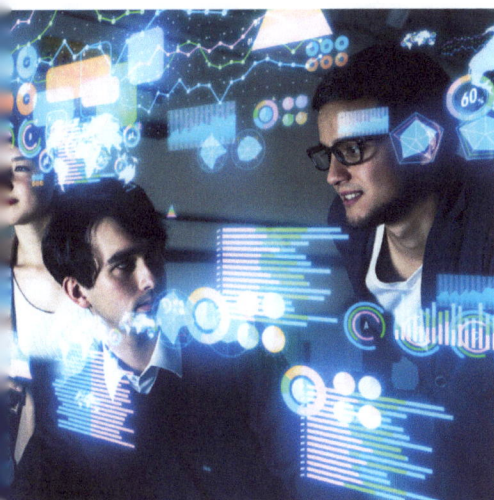

Overcoming Challenges: Navigating a Dynamic Landscape

While innovative marketing strategies offer many opportunities, they also come with challenges. The rapidly changing digital landscape, evolving consumer expectations, and increasing competition can be daunting.

Staying informed and adaptable is essential. Continuously monitor industry trends, technological advancements, and changes in consumer behavior.

Experimentation can help you discover what works best for your brand and audience. Be willing to try new approaches, measure results, and adjust as needed.

Resource constraints, such as budget and staffing, can also be a challenge. Prioritize initiatives that offer the highest potential return on investment and consider outsourcing or automation to maximize efficiency.

Maintaining authenticity and trust is another challenge. Consumers are increasingly skeptical of overt marketing tactics. Focus on building genuine relationships and providing real value.

By approaching challenges with a proactive and solution-oriented mindset, you can navigate the complexities of the marketing landscape and position your brand for success

Reaching and engaging with your target audience has never been more important or more challenging. The evolving marketing landscape demands creativity, adaptability, and a deep understanding of your audience's needs and preferences.

By embracing innovative marketing strategies such as content marketing, influencer partnerships, social media engagement, email marketing, personalization, emerging technologies, experiential marketing, and strategic partnerships, businesses can connect with their audience in meaningful and impactful ways.

Data analytics provides the insights needed to inform and refine your strategies, while a focus on customer experience ensures loyalty and advocacy. Overcoming challenges requires a commitment to continuous learning, experimentation, and authenticity.

Marketing is not a one-size-fits-all endeavor. It is a dynamic and ongoing process that requires flexibility, creativity, and a willingness to evolve. By staying informed, leveraging the right tools and techniques, and maintaining a customer-centric approach, businesses can effectively reach their target audience and drive growth and success.

The journey toward marketing excellence is an exciting and rewarding one. Start today by assessing your current strategies, identifying opportunities for innovation, and taking bold steps toward creating meaningful connections with your audience. Your brand's future success depends on it.

Scaling Your Business Without Breaking the Bank: Cost-Effective Strategies for Growth

Scaling a business is one of the most rewarding phases in the entrepreneurial journey. It signals that your product or service is resonating with customers, and that you are ready to take things to the next level. However, growth often brings new complexities, including increased operational demands, expanded marketing efforts, and a greater need for structure. For many businesses, especially small to mid-sized ones, the biggest question becomes how to grow effectively without overwhelming available resources.

The common belief is that scaling requires massive investments in staffing, infrastructure, and advertising. While these factors can certainly play a role in growth, they are not the only path forward. In fact, many successful businesses have found ways to scale smartly by being resourceful, strategic, and focused on what truly moves the needle. Financial discipline and creative problem-solving often matter just as much as

budget size.

It is important to understand that scaling is not just about doing more. It is about doing more of what works and doing it better. By identifying your core strengths, streamlining processes, and leveraging tools and partnerships wisely, you can unlock growth opportunities without draining your bank account. The key is to stay lean while maintaining quality, efficiency, and customer satisfaction.

In this article, we will explore cost-effective strategies that can help you scale your business with confidence. From automating repetitive tasks to maximizing your existing customer base, these approaches are designed to help you grow steadily while keeping your financial foundation strong. Whether you are just starting to scale or looking to optimize your current growth strategy, these insights will offer practical steps you can put into action right away.

DOING GOOD IS GOOD BUSINESS

SHARING THE CREDIT

Your business can give to charity without writing a check. Visit **www.SharingTheCredit.com** and start giving today.

Set Achievable and Realistic Goals

Setting achievable and realistic goals is a critical first step towards scaling your business. Without clear goals in place, you risk losing focus and direction, which can lead to wasted resources and stalled growth. In this section, we'll explore the importance of setting achievable and realistic goals, how to set them, and how to measure your progress towards achieving them.

Importance of Setting Achievable and Realistic Goals

Setting achievable and realistic goals is essential because it helps you focus your efforts and resources towards a clear direction. It also gives you a benchmark against which you can measure your progress and adjust your strategies accordingly.

By setting achievable goals, you can build momentum, stay motivated, and achieve sustainable growth over time.

How to Set Achievable and Realistic Goals for Your Business

To set achievable and realistic goals, you need to consider your business's current state, future aspirations, and external factors that may impact your growth. Here are some steps to follow:

- **Evaluate your current state:** Assess your business's current strengths, weaknesses, opportunities, and threats (SWOT analysis). This will help you identify areas that require improvement and opportunities for growth.

- **Define your vision and mission:** Your vision and mission statements should be aligned with your goals and reflect your long-term aspirations for your business.

- **Identify specific objectives:** Break down your long-term goals into specific, measurable objectives that are achievable within a reasonable timeframe. Make sure your objectives are specific, measurable, achievable, relevant, and time-bound (SMART).

- **Prioritize your objectives:** Determine which objectives are most important and prioritize them based on their potential impact on your business's growth.

- **Develop a plan:** Create a roadmap that outlines the steps you need to take to achieve your objectives. Make sure your plan is realistic and achievable within your available resources.

How to Measure Your Progress Towards Your Goals

To measure your progress towards your goals, you need to establish key performance indicators (KPIs) that will help you track your progress. Your KPIs should be aligned with your objectives and reflect your business's performance.

Here are some examples of KPIs:

- **Revenue growth:** Monitor your revenue growth over time and set targets for each quarter or year.

- **Customer acquisition:** Track the number of new customers you acquire each month or quarter.

- **Customer retention:** Measure your customer retention rate and set targets for improving it over time.

- **Website traffic:** Monitor your website traffic and track the sources of traffic to identify areas for improvement.

- **Employee productivity:** Monitor your employees' productivity and set targets for improving their performance over time.

By setting achievable and realistic goals and measuring your progress towards achieving them, you can build momentum, stay motivated, and achieve sustainable growth over time.

Optimize Your Processes and Procedures

Optimizing your processes and procedures is another crucial step towards scaling your business. Inefficiencies in your business processes can waste valuable resources, reduce productivity, and limit your growth potential. In this section, we'll explore the importance of optimizing your processes and procedures, how to analyze them, and ways to optimize them to reduce costs and increase efficiency.

Importance of Optimizing Processes and Procedures

Optimizing your processes and procedures is essential because it helps you streamline your operations, reduce costs, and increase efficiency. It also enables you to identify and eliminate bottlenecks that may hinder your growth potential. By optimizing your processes, you can improve your customer experience, increase your capacity, and achieve sustainable growth over time.

How to Analyze Your Business Processes to Identify Inefficiencies

To identify inefficiencies in your business processes, you need to take a close look at how you do things.

Here are some steps to follow:

- **Map out your processes:** Create a visual representation of your business processes to help you identify the steps involved and how they relate to each other.

- **Identify bottlenecks:** Determine which steps in your processes are slowing you down or causing delays. Look for areas where work piles up, wait times are long, or errors occur.

- **Analyze your data:** Collect data on your processes to identify trends, patterns, and areas for improvement. Look for metrics such as cycle time, lead time, and throughput.

- **Get feedback:** Ask your employees, customers, and suppliers for feedback on your processes. They may have insights into areas that need improvement.

Ways to Optimize Your Processes to Reduce Costs and Increase Efficiency

Once you've identified inefficiencies in your processes, you need to optimize them to reduce costs and increase efficiency. Here are some ways to do that:

1. **Automate processes:** Use technology to automate repetitive tasks and eliminate manual processes. This can save you time and reduce the risk of errors.

2. **Simplify processes:** Streamline your processes by removing unnecessary steps, consolidating tasks, or reorganizing your workflows.

3. **Standardize processes:** Develop standard operating procedures (SOPs) to ensure consistency and reduce the risk of errors.

4. **Train your employees:** Provide training and support to your employees to help them understand and implement your optimized processes effectively.

By optimizing your processes and procedures, you can reduce costs, increase efficiency, and achieve sustainable growth over time. It requires a continuous effort to identify and eliminate inefficiencies, but the benefits are well worth the investment.

Embrace Technology

Embracing technology is another critical step towards scaling your business. In today's digital age, technology plays a vital role in every aspect of business operations. By leveraging the latest technologies, you can improve your productivity, reduce costs, and enhance your customer experience. In this section, we'll explore the importance of embracing technology, how to evaluate technology solutions, and ways to implement technology in your business.

Importance of Embracing Technology

Embracing technology is essential because it can help you automate your processes, reduce costs, and increase efficiency.

It can also help you reach a wider audience, expand your customer base, and improve your customer experience. By embracing technology, you can stay competitive, adapt to changing market conditions, and achieve sustainable growth over time.

How to Evaluate Technology Solutions

To evaluate technology solutions for your business, you need to consider several factors, such as your business needs, budget, and existing infrastructure. Here are some steps to follow:

1. **Identify your business needs:** Determine which areas of your business could benefit from technology solutions. Look for opportunities to automate processes, improve communication, and enhance customer experience.

2. Research technology solutions: Research technology solutions that meet your business needs. Look for solutions that are scalable, affordable, and easy to implement.

3. Evaluate the costs: Consider the costs of implementing technology solutions, such as upfront costs, ongoing costs, and training costs. Make sure the benefits outweigh the costs.

4. Test the solutions: Test the technology solutions to ensure they meet your business needs and are easy to use. Consider conducting a pilot project before fully implementing the solutions.

Ways to Implement Technology in Tour Business

Once you've identified technology solutions that meet your business needs, you need to implement them effectively.

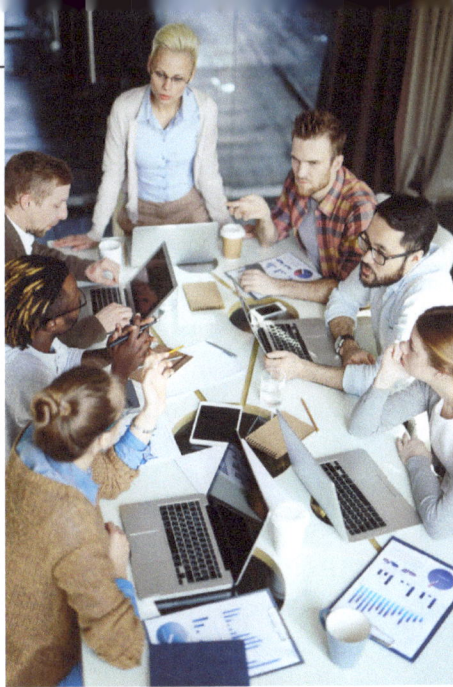

Here are some ways to do that:

1. Integrate your systems: Integrate your technology solutions with your existing systems to streamline your operations and reduce manual processes.

2. Provide training: Provide training and support to your employees to help them understand and use the technology solutions effectively.

3. Monitor your performance: Monitor your performance metrics to ensure your technology solutions are delivering the expected results. Make adjustments as necessary to improve performance.

4. Stay up to date: Stay up to date with the latest technology trends and innovations to remain competitive and identify new opportunities for growth.

By embracing technology, you can automate your processes, reduce costs, and increase efficiency. It requires a continuous effort to identify and implement new technology solutions, but the benefits are well worth the investment.

Outsource Tasks

Outsourcing tasks is another cost-effective strategy for scaling your business. Outsourcing refers to the process of hiring external contractors or agencies to handle specific tasks or functions for your business. By outsourcing, you can tap into specialized expertise, reduce labor costs, and focus on core business activities. In this section, we'll explore the benefits of outsourcing, how to identify tasks to outsource, and how to choose the right outsourcing partners.

Benefits of Outsourcing

Outsourcing provides several benefits for businesses, including:

1. Access to specialized expertise: Outsourcing allows you to access specialized expertise that may not be available in-house. You can hire experts in specific fields, such as accounting, marketing, or IT, to handle tasks that require specialized skills.

2. Cost savings: Outsourcing can be more cost-effective than hiring full-time employees. You can avoid the costs of benefits, taxes, and training associated with full-time employees.

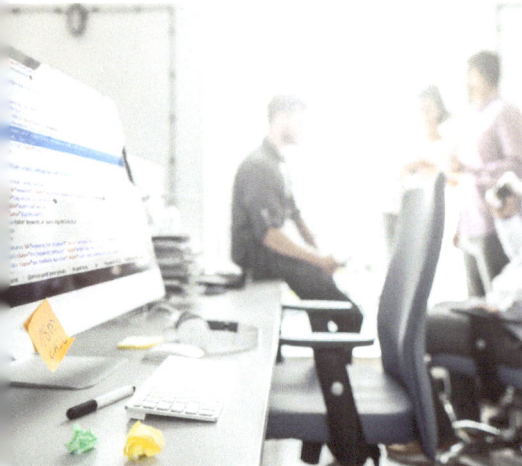

3. Increased flexibility: Outsourcing provides you with flexibility in terms of staffing. You can hire contractors or agencies on a project-by-project basis, allowing you to scale up or down as needed.

4. Focus on core activities: Outsourcing allows you to focus on core business activities while external contractors handle non-core functions. This can improve your productivity and help you achieve your growth objectives.

Identifying Tasks to Outsource

To identify tasks to outsource, you need to consider which tasks are non-core functions that can be handled by external contractors.

Here are some steps to follow:

1. Evaluate your business processes: Evaluate your business processes to identify tasks that are not core functions. Look for tasks that are time-consuming, repetitive, or require specialized expertise.

2. Consider the benefits of outsourcing: Consider the benefits of outsourcing specific tasks, such as cost savings, access to specialized expertise, and increased flexibility.

3. Determine your outsourcing requirements: Determine your outsourcing requirements, such as the scope of work, budget, and timeline.

Choosing the Right Outsourcing Partner

Choosing the right outsourcing partner is essential for the success of your outsourcing strategy. Here are some factors to consider when choosing an outsourcing partner:

1. Expertise: Choose an outsourcing partner with expertise in the specific task or function you want to outsource.

2. Reputation: Choose an outsourcing partner with a good reputation in the industry. Look for reviews and testimonials from previous clients.

3. Communication: Choose an outsourcing partner that communicates effectively and regularly. Clear communication is essential for the success of your outsourcing project.

4. Cost: Choose an outsourcing partner that provides cost-effective solutions without compromising on quality.

Outsourcing tasks is a cost-effective strategy for scaling your business. It allows you to access specialized expertise, reduce labor costs, and focus on core business activities. By identifying tasks to outsource and choosing the right outsourcing partners, you can achieve sustainable growth over time.

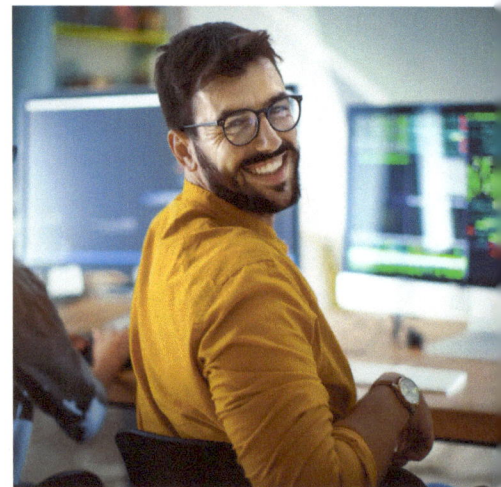

Invest in Employee Development

Investing in employee development is another cost-effective strategy for scaling your business. Employee development refers to the process of providing employees

with opportunities to learn new skills, improve their performance, and advance their careers. By investing in employee development, you can improve your employee retention rates, enhance your team's capabilities, and increase your business's productivity. In this section, we'll explore the benefits of investing in employee development, how to identify employee development needs, and how to create effective employee development programs.

Benefits of Investing in Employee Development

Investing in employee development provides several benefits for businesses, including:

1. Improved employee retention rates: Investing in employee development shows your employees that you are invested in their careers and value their contributions. This can increase your employee retention rates and reduce the costs associated with employee turnover.

2. Enhanced team capabilities: Employee development can enhance your team's capabilities and improve their performance. This can lead to increased productivity, better quality work, and improved customer satisfaction.

3. Increased innovation: Employee development can provide your team with the skills and knowledge needed to innovate and develop new products or services. This can help you stay ahead of the competition and grow your business.

Identifying employee development needs

To identify employee development needs, you need to consider the skills and knowledge required to perform specific job functions. Here are some steps to follow:

1. Conduct a skills assessment: Conduct a skills assessment to identify skills gaps within your team. This can help you identify areas where employee development is needed.

2. Review job descriptions: Review job descriptions to identify the skills and knowledge required for specific job functions.

3. Solicit employee feedback: Solicit feedback from your employees to identify their career goals and development needs.

Creating effective employee development programs

To create effective employee development programs, you need to consider the specific needs of your team and business. Here are some steps to follow:

1. Set clear objectives: Set clear objectives for your employee development program. This can help you measure the success of the program and ensure that it aligns with your business goals.

2. Choose appropriate training methods: Choose appropriate training methods that match the learning styles of your employees. This can include on-the-job training, workshops, online courses, and mentoring.

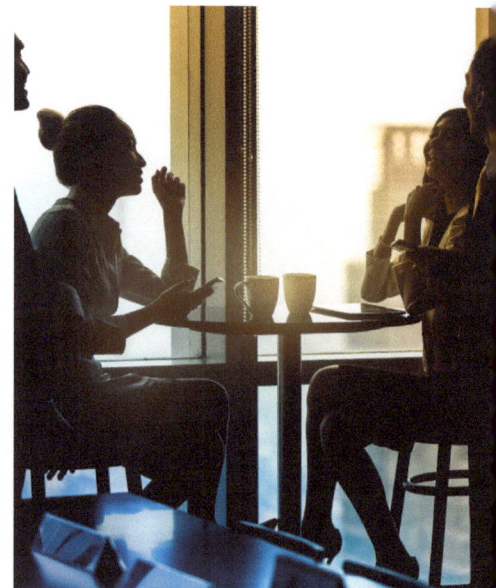

3. Provide ongoing support:
Provide ongoing support for your employees as they participate in the development program. This can include coaching, feedback, and additional resources.

Investing in employee development is one of the most cost-effective and impactful strategies for scaling a business. When you prioritize the growth of your team, you build a foundation for long-term success. Training and development programs not only enhance your employees' skills but also improve job satisfaction and retention. This reduces turnover costs and ensures that your team continues to evolve with the needs of the business. A well-developed workforce is more capable of handling increased responsibilities, solving complex problems, and contributing to innovation.

By identifying skill gaps and tailoring development initiatives to meet those needs, you empower your employees to grow alongside your company. This creates a culture of continuous improvement and accountability. Rather than constantly hiring externally to meet new challenges, you can promote from within, which saves time, strengthens morale, and preserves institutional knowledge. Ultimately, a motivated and skilled team becomes a driving force behind sustainable business growth.

Scaling your business often feels overwhelming and expensive, but it does not have to be. The key is to focus on smart, sustainable growth rather than rapid expansion at all costs. Start by setting clear, realistic goals that align with your resources and long-term vision. Evaluate your current operations to identify inefficiencies and look for opportunities to streamline processes. Embracing the right technology can help automate repetitive tasks, reduce manual labor, and increase productivity without the need for major investments. Outsourcing non-core functions is another way to save money while maintaining focus on what matters most. These foundational steps can create a lean, scalable framework that supports steady growth.

Beyond operations, consider growth strategies that deliver high impact with low overhead. Implementing referral programs can tap into your existing customer base to drive new business.

Leveraging social media allows you to build brand awareness and engage with customers without a large advertising budget.

Investing in employee development ensures your team is equipped to grow with the company and take on more responsibility as you scale. Scaling is not a sprint but a journey that requires consistent effort, adaptability, and patience.

By applying these cost-effective strategies and staying focused on sustainable growth, your business can expand confidently without putting your financial stability at risk.

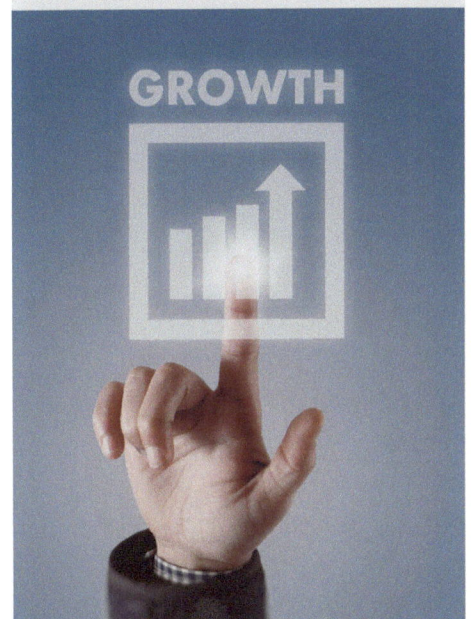

The Power of Analytics: How Data Drives Business Decisions

Successful businesses are no longer guided by instinct alone. While experience and intuition still have their place, they must be supported by reliable evidence and real-time insights to stay competitive and make informed decisions. Data has become one of the most valuable resources available to organizations across every industry. It helps uncover patterns, track performance, and reveal opportunities that might otherwise go unnoticed.

The power of analytics lies in its ability to transform raw information into clear, actionable insight. Companies that invest in analytics gain a deeper understanding of their operations and customers, allowing them to anticipate trends and make decisions with greater confidence. Analytics is no longer just a tool—it is a strategic cornerstone for sustainable growth.

This article explores how data and analytics have reshaped business decision-making. It will examine how organizations gather and interpret data, the advantages of a data-driven approach, the challenges they may encounter, and the strategies needed to implement analytics successfully.

The Role of Data in Business Decision-Making

Data is the fuel that powers modern decision-making. Every interaction with customers, every transaction, and every operational process generates data that can be collected and analyzed. By systematically gathering and interpreting this information, businesses can make decisions that are not only timely but also backed by evidence.

Collecting and Organizing Data

The first step in using data for decision-making is collecting and organizing it. Businesses draw data from a wide range of sources. Internal data might include sales records, website analytics, customer service logs, and inventory levels. External data sources can include market research, competitor analysis, social media activity, and publicly available economic indicators.

Organizing this data requires robust systems and processes. Data must be stored in a way that allows for easy retrieval and analysis. Poor data organization can lead to inefficiencies and inaccuracies that undermine the decision-making process.

Analyzing and Interpreting Data

Once data is collected and organized, it must be analyzed. This involves applying statistical techniques and using software tools to identify patterns, trends, and correlations. Common methods include regression analysis, clustering, and time-series analysis.

Interpretation is the next critical step. Raw numbers are rarely useful on their own. Businesses must translate the results of data analysis into actionable insights. This requires an understanding of both the data itself and the broader business context in which it exists.

Extracting Insights

The goal of data analysis is to extract insights that inform decisions. These insights can reveal customer preferences, operational inefficiencies, market trends, and much more. By understanding what the data is telling them, businesses can make decisions that align with their strategic goals and respond proactively to challenges and opportunities.

Enhancing Accuracy and Objectivity

Data-driven decisions are typically more accurate and objective than those based on intuition alone. Data helps to eliminate biases and emotions from the decision-making process. It allows businesses to test assumptions, validate hypotheses, and measure outcomes in a systematic way.

Driving Efficiency and Productivity

Analyzing operational data can reveal inefficiencies and bottlenecks. By addressing these issues, businesses can improve productivity and reduce costs. Data-driven insights can also inform resource allocation, ensuring that time, money, and effort are directed toward the most impactful activities.

Understanding Customers

Data provides a window into customer behavior. By analyzing data from sales transactions, website visits, social media interactions, and customer feedback, businesses can gain a deep understanding of what their customers want and need. This understanding can inform product development, marketing strategies, and customer service improvements.

Gaining a Competitive Advantage

Organizations that leverage data effectively can gain a significant competitive advantage. They can respond to market changes more quickly, identify emerging trends, and develop innovative products and services that meet customer needs better than those of their competitors.

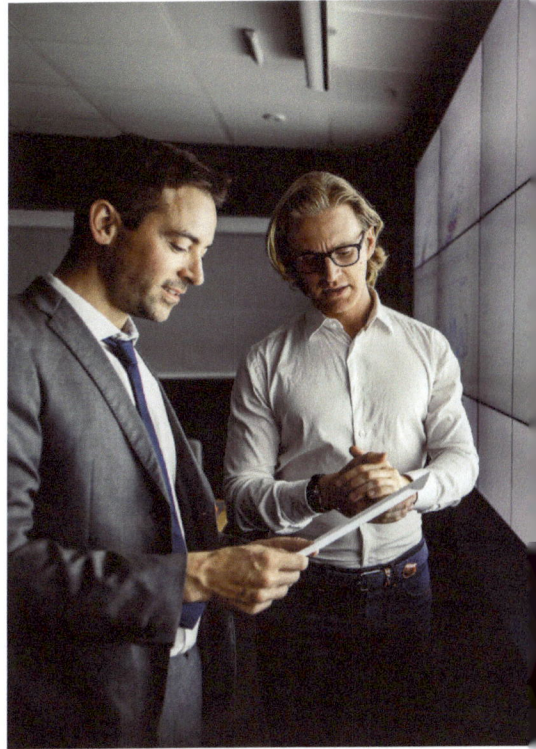

Key Benefits of Data-Driven Decision-Making

The advantages of using data to guide decisions are substantial. Organizations that adopt a data-driven approach often experience improvements across multiple dimensions of their business.

Improved Accuracy and Objectivity

Data-driven decisions reduce the influence of personal biases and gut feelings. By relying on empirical evidence, businesses can make more accurate and objective choices that lead to better outcomes.

Greater Efficiency and Productivity

Data analysis can identify areas where processes can be streamlined or automated. This can lead to significant improvements in efficiency and productivity, reducing costs and freeing up resources for other initiatives.

Enhanced Customer Understanding

By analyzing customer data, businesses can gain insights into purchasing patterns, preferences, and pain points. This enables them to tailor their offerings and marketing efforts to better meet customer needs, enhancing satisfaction and loyalty.

Competitive Advantage

Data-driven organizations can respond more quickly to market changes and customer demands. They are also better positioned to identify new opportunities and mitigate risks, giving them a competitive edge.

Informed Strategic Planning

Data provides the foundation for informed strategic planning. By analyzing trends and forecasting future conditions, businesses can develop strategies that position them for long-term success.

Risk Mitigation

Data can help businesses identify and assess risks. By analyzing historical data and monitoring current trends, organizations can anticipate potential challenges and develop contingency plans.

Encouraging Innovation

A data-driven approach encourages experimentation and innovation. Businesses can test new ideas, measure the results, and iterate based on what the data reveals. This fosters a culture of continuous improvement.

Challenges and Considerations in Data-Driven Decision-Making

While the benefits of data-driven decision-making are clear, implementing this approach is not without its challenges.

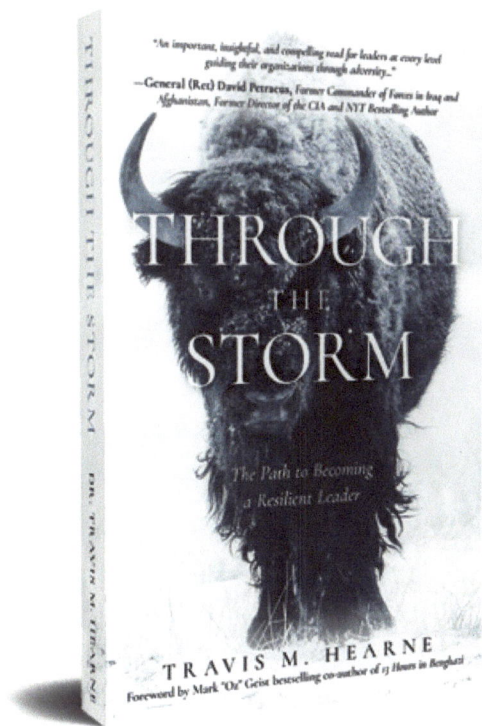

Data Privacy and Security

With the collection and use of data comes the responsibility to protect it. Businesses must ensure that they comply with data privacy regulations and take steps to safeguard sensitive information from unauthorized access or breaches.

Data Quality and Bias

The quality of the data used in decision-making is critical. Inaccurate, incomplete, or biased data can lead to flawed insights and poor decisions. Businesses must implement processes to ensure data accuracy and address potential biases in data collection and analysis.

Skill Gaps

Effective data analysis requires specialized skills. Many organizations face a shortage of employees with the necessary expertise in data science, statistics, and analytics. Investing in training and hiring skilled professionals is essential.

Ethical Considerations

Using data responsibly involves ethical considerations. Businesses must ensure that they use data in ways that respect customer privacy and avoid discriminatory practices.

Integration and Complexity

Many organizations collect data from multiple sources that may not be easily integrated. Managing and analyzing data across different systems can be complex and resource-intensive.

Managing Big Data

As the volume of data grows, businesses need scalable infrastructure and advanced tools to manage and analyze large datasets effectively.

Continuous Improvement

Data-driven decision-making is an ongoing process. Businesses must continuously monitor and evaluate their data practices, update their strategies, and adapt to changing conditions.

Implementing Data-Driven Decision-Making

Adopting a data-driven approach involves more than just collecting data. It requires a cultural shift and the implementation of systems and practices that support the effective use of data in decision-making.

Fostering a Data-Driven Culture

Organizations must cultivate a culture that values data and encourages its use in decision-making at all levels. This involves promoting data literacy, encouraging curiosity, and rewarding evidence-based decision-making.

Investing in Technology

Choosing the right analytics tools and technologies is essential. Businesses should invest in data management systems, visualization tools, and advanced analytics platforms that meet their needs.

Building a Skilled Team

Hiring data professionals and providing training for existing employees can help organizations build the skills needed to analyze and interpret data effectively.

Establishing Data Governance

Clear roles, responsibilities, and processes for data management must be established. This includes setting standards for data quality, privacy, and security.

Embracing an Iterative Approach

Data-driven decision-making should be seen as an iterative process. Businesses should start with small-scale initiatives, learn from the results, and refine their strategies over time.

Encouraging Collaboration

Breaking down silos and fostering collaboration between departments that generate and use data can enhance the quality and impact of data-driven decisions.

Communicating and Managing Change

Change management is critical. Businesses must communicate the benefits of data-driven decision-making and address any concerns through transparent communication.

Advanced Strategies for Leveraging Analytics

While basic data collection and analysis can yield valuable insights, businesses that want to fully capitalize on the power of analytics must adopt more advanced strategies. These approaches enable deeper insights, predictive capabilities, and more sophisticated decision-making.

Predictive Analytics

Predictive analytics uses historical data to forecast future outcomes. By applying statistical models and machine learning algorithms, businesses can predict customer behavior, market trends, and operational risks. This allows for proactive decision-making rather than reactive responses.

For example, a retail company might use predictive analytics to forecast which products will be in high demand during an upcoming season. This can inform inventory management, marketing campaigns, and supply chain planning.

Prescriptive Analytics

Prescriptive analytics goes a step further by not only predicting outcomes but also recommending actions to achieve desired results. This approach uses optimization and simulation algorithms to identify the best course of action based on data insights.

For instance, a logistics company might use prescriptive analytics to determine the most efficient delivery routes while considering factors like traffic patterns, fuel costs, and delivery deadlines.

Real-Time Analytics

Real-time analytics involves analyzing data as it is generated, allowing for immediate insights and action. This is particularly valuable in industries where timing is critical, such as finance, healthcare, and e-commerce.

A financial trading firm, for example, might use real-time analytics to monitor market fluctuations and execute trades automatically based on predefined criteria. Similarly, an e-commerce platform can use real-time data to personalize recommendations for shoppers.

Customer Segmentation

Advanced analytics enables businesses to segment their customer base into distinct groups based on behavior, demographics, and preferences. This allows for more targeted marketing, personalized experiences, and improved customer retention.

A travel company might segment customers based on travel habits, preferred destinations, and spending patterns, allowing them to offer tailored vacation packages that resonate with each segment.

Sentiment Analysis

Sentiment analysis involves analyzing text data from sources like social media, reviews, and customer feedback to understand public sentiment about a brand, product, or service. This can provide valuable insights into customer perceptions and help businesses address issues or capitalize on positive trends.

A software company might use sentiment analysis to monitor user feedback on product updates, allowing them to identify and address concerns quickly.

Real-World Case Studies

To illustrate the transformative power of analytics, let's examine how leading companies have successfully integrated data-driven decision-making into their operations.

Amazon

Amazon is a pioneer in leveraging data to drive decision-making. The company collects vast amounts of data on customer behavior, purchase history, and browsing patterns. This data informs product recommendations, inventory management, pricing strategies, and even the design of new products.

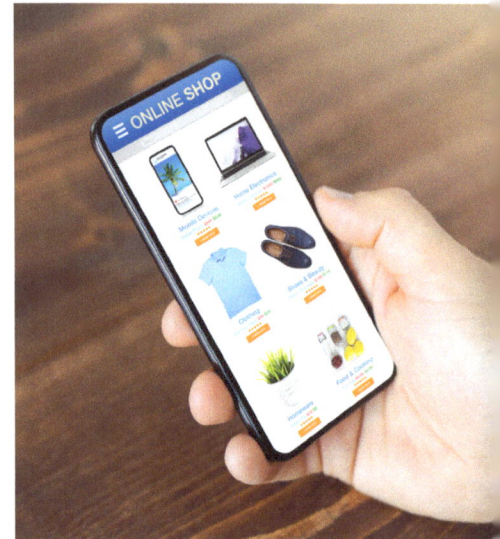

Amazon's recommendation engine, which accounts for a significant portion of the company's revenue, uses collaborative filtering and predictive analytics to suggest products that customers are likely to purchase. This personalized approach enhances the customer experience and drives sales.

Netflix

Netflix uses data analytics to make decisions about content creation, recommendation algorithms, and user experience.

By analyzing viewing habits, search queries, and user ratings, Netflix can predict which types of content will be popular with different segments of its audience.

This data-driven approach has guided the development of original content like "House of Cards" and "Stranger Things," both of which were informed by insights into viewer preferences.

Procter & Gamble

Procter & Gamble (P&G) has embraced analytics to improve product development, marketing, and supply chain management. The company uses data to understand consumer needs, optimize product formulations, and predict market trends.

P&G's supply chain operations benefit from real-time data analytics that monitor production, inventory, and distribution. This allows the company to respond quickly to changes in demand and minimize disruptions.

Starbucks

Starbucks leverages data analytics to enhance customer engagement and optimize store operations. The company's loyalty program collects data on customer purchases, preferences, and feedback.

This data informs personalized marketing campaigns, product recommendations, and promotional offers. Starbucks also uses analytics to determine the best locations for new stores based on factors like foot traffic, demographic trends, and competitive analysis.

The Future of Data-Driven Decision-Making

As technology continues to evolve, the role of data in business decision-making will only grow more significant. Several trends are shaping the future of analytics.

Artificial Intelligence and Machine Learning

Artificial intelligence (AI) and machine learning are driving the next wave of analytics innovation. These technologies enable businesses to analyze larger and more complex datasets, automate decision-making, and uncover insights

that would be difficult or impossible to identify manually.

AI-powered analytics can enhance predictive and prescriptive capabilities, allowing businesses to anticipate trends and respond with greater agility.

Internet of Things (IoT)

The proliferation of IoT devices is generating massive amounts of data. Businesses can harness this data to monitor equipment performance, track supply chain activities, and gain insights into customer behavior.

For example, manufacturers can use IoT data to predict equipment maintenance needs, reducing downtime and improving efficiency.

Data Democratization

Data democratization refers to making data and analytics tools accessible to employees across all levels of an organization. By empowering more people to use data in their daily work, businesses can foster a culture of data-driven decision-making.

Self-service analytics platforms and intuitive data visualization tools are making it easier for non-technical users to access and interpret data.

Privacy and Ethical Considerations

As data collection and analysis become more pervasive, businesses must navigate privacy and ethical challenges. Regulations like the General Data Protection Regulation (GDPR) and the California Consumer Privacy Act (CCPA) impose strict requirements on how data is collected, stored, and used.

Businesses must prioritize transparency, obtain consent when collecting data, and implement robust security measures to protect sensitive information.

The Rise of Data Literacy

To fully leverage the power of analytics, organizations must invest in building data literacy across their workforce. This involves training employees to understand data, ask the right questions, and interpret analytics results accurately.

Data literacy will become an essential skill in the modern workplace, enabling employees to make informed decisions and contribute to data-driven initiatives.

The power of analytics in driving business decisions cannot be overstated. In an environment where competition is fierce and change is constant, data provides the clarity and confidence needed to navigate uncertainty and seize opportunities.

By collecting, analyzing, and interpreting data, businesses can gain valuable insights into their operations, customers, and markets. Data-driven decision-making enhances accuracy, efficiency, and innovation while reducing risks and enabling more

strategic planning. Implementing a data-driven approach requires commitment, investment, and cultural change. Organizations must address challenges related to data privacy, quality, and skills while fostering a culture that values evidence-based decision-making

Advanced analytics strategies such as predictive modeling, prescriptive analytics, real-time analysis, and customer segmentation offer powerful tools for gaining deeper insights and making proactive decisions. Real-world examples from leading companies like Amazon, Netflix, Procter & Gamble, and Starbucks demonstrate the transformative impact of analytics.

Looking ahead, emerging technologies like artificial intelligence, machine learning, and the Internet of Things will continue to expand the possibilities of data-driven decision-making. Businesses that embrace these innovations and invest in data literacy will be well-positioned to thrive in the data-driven future.

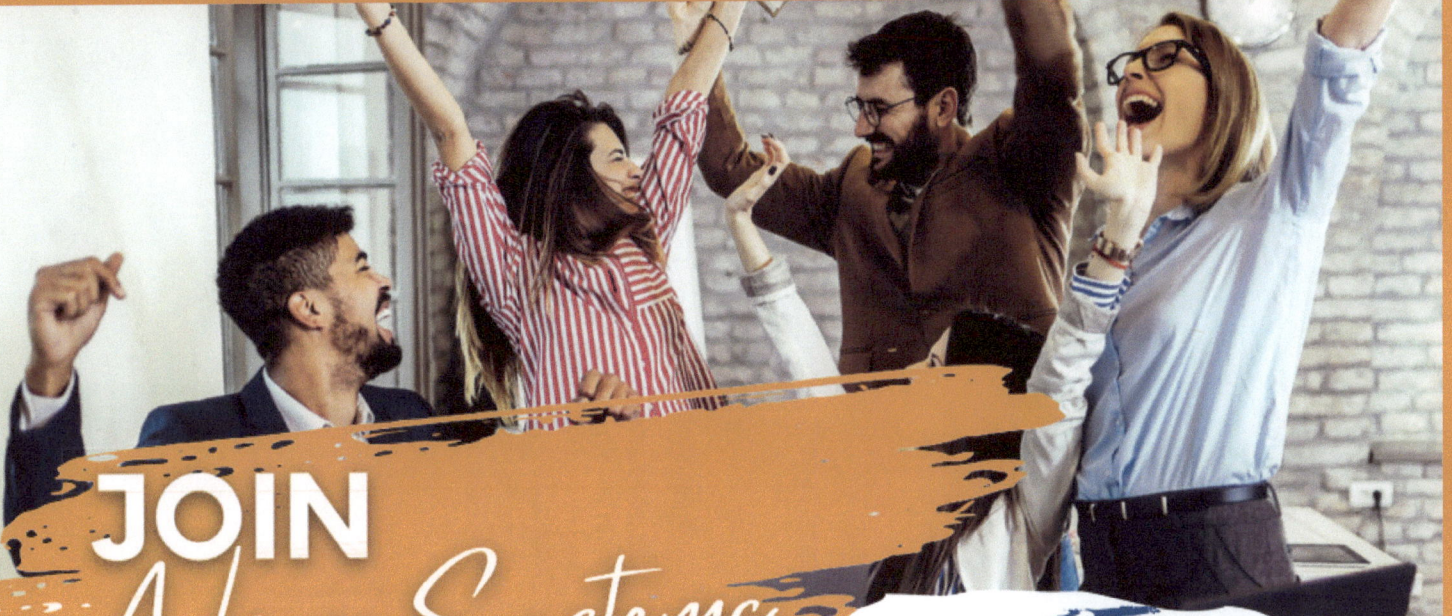

JOIN
Achieve Systems

BECOME AN ACHIEVE SYSTEMS MEMBER TODAY!

Education
We help you get the tools to create a thriving business! It's turnkey, you can start NOW!

Marketing
We provide marketing guidelines but also plug you into our conferences, events and database

Community
We have a thriving community of entrepreneurs and business owners for you to collaborate, refer and partner with to grow and up-level your business!

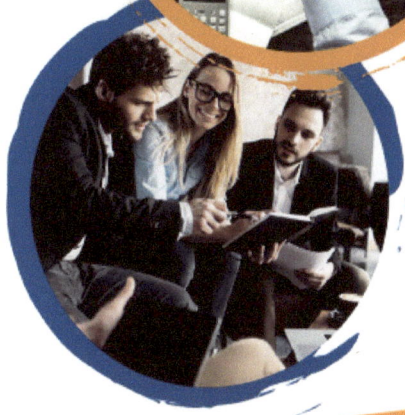

WE WORK WITH ENTREPRENEURS, BUSINESS OWNERS, SPEAKERS & LEADERS!

CONTACT US OR REGISTER HERE: www.AchieveSystemsPro.com

In summary, data has evolved from being a passive byproduct of day-to-day operations into a powerful strategic asset that can shape the direction and success of an entire organization. When managed and analyzed effectively, data provides clarity in decision-making, uncovers hidden opportunities, and offers a deeper understanding of both internal performance and external market conditions. It enables businesses to move beyond assumptions and act with greater precision and confidence. In an increasingly competitive landscape, the ability to harness data is no longer a luxury but a necessity for those looking to drive meaningful, long-term growth.

Becoming a truly data-driven organization requires more than adopting new tools or hiring analysts. It involves a cultural shift that prioritizes evidence-based thinking, continuous learning, and cross-functional collaboration. The path may come with challenges, such as addressing skill gaps, ensuring data quality, and overcoming resistance to change. However, the payoff is substantial. Businesses that fully commit to leveraging analytics are not only more agile and resilient but are also better prepared to anticipate trends, serve their customers more effectively, and lead confidently in an ever-evolving market.

Mastering the Art of Client Acquisition

Standing out in the coaching industry is not always easy. With more coaches entering the field every day, the competition for clients has become increasingly fierce. Many talented professionals find themselves wondering how to get noticed, how to communicate their value, and how to consistently attract the right people to their services. It is easy to feel overwhelmed by the sheer number of options available and the evolving expectations of modern clients.

Yet attracting clients does not have to feel like an impossible task. With the right mindset and tools, building a steady stream of clients becomes less about chasing and more about positioning. The key lies in being intentional about your approach. Rather than relying on scattered tactics, successful coaches develop a clear, strategic process that aligns with who they are and the people they serve best. This approach not only saves time but also builds credibility and trust with potential clients.

Whether you are just starting out or have years of experience behind you, there is always room to grow and refine your client acquisition skills. The needs of your audience change, the platforms they use evolve, and the way people make decisions continues to shift. Remaining open to learning and adapting is one of the most powerful traits you can bring to your business. This is especially true in a service-based industry where relationships and trust are everything.

This guide is designed to help you cut through the noise. It is not about gimmicks or one-size-fits-all solutions. Instead, it offers a practical and grounded approach to building a client base that is both loyal and aligned with your values. From understanding your niche to refining your message and improving your visibility, each step in the process will help you move forward with clarity and purpose.

By the time you finish this guide, you will have a stronger foundation for attracting clients

who are a great fit for your coaching style. More than that, you will be able to approach client acquisition with confidence, knowing that you have the tools and understanding to grow your practice in a sustainable and meaningful way. The art of client acquisition is not about selling. It is about connection, value, and service. And with the right strategy in place, it becomes a natural extension of the work you love to do.

Defining Client Acquisition

Client acquisition, at its core, refers to the process of gaining new clients or customers for your business. In the context of coaching, it involves attracting individuals or organizations that require your coaching services, convincing them of your value,

and converting them into paying clients.

Why is Client Acquisition Important?

Effective client acquisition is essential in the coaching industry for several reasons. Firstly, it directly contributes to your revenue stream. More clients equate to more business, which translates to higher income.

Secondly, client acquisition helps in expanding your coaching practice. As you gain more clients, your reach and influence in the coaching industry increase, paving the way for further opportunities.

Lastly, successful client acquisition boosts your brand reputation. Satisfied clients can become ambassadors of your services, referring you to others in their network and thus organically driving your business growth.

SEO Strategies for Client Acquisition

Now that we've covered the basics, let's move to actionable strategies. One of the most effective ways to improve client acquisition in the digital era is by leveraging Search Engine Optimization (SEO). When used correctly, SEO can help your coaching business appear in front of the right people at the

exact moment they are searching for the solutions you offer.

Here are a few SEO strategies to boost your online visibility and attract more clients:

- **Keyword Optimization:** Identify and use relevant keywords that your potential clients are likely to use when searching for coaching services. Incorporate these keywords into your website content, blog posts, and meta descriptions.

- **Quality Content:** Publish high-quality, valuable content that resonates with your target audience. This not only helps in ranking higher on search engine results but also establishes you as a credible authority in your field.

- **Backlink Building:** Backlinks, or inbound links from other websites, signal to search engines that your content is valuable and trustworthy. Seek opportunities to generate quality backlinks through guest blogging, collaborations, and testimonials.

- **Website Optimization:** Ensure your website is user-friendly, mobile-responsive, and fast. A well-optimized website enhances the user experience, increasing the chances of visitors converting into clients.

How to Identify Your Ideal Client

Understanding who your ideal client is constitutes a critical part of a successful coaching practice. It allows you to tailor your services, marketing strategies, and communication to appeal directly to the people most likely to engage with your business. Here's a step-by-step guide to help you identify your ideal client.

Step 1: Define Your Coaching Niche

Before you can identify your ideal client, you need to have a clear understanding of your coaching niche. Are you a life coach, a career coach, an executive coach, or do you specialize in another area? Defining your niche will provide a solid foundation for determining who your services will benefit the most.

Step 2: Understand Their Demographics

Demographic details are the basics of your ideal client profile. Consider aspects like age, gender, location, income level, and educational background. For instance, if you're an executive coach, your ideal client may be a C-suite professional in their late 40s, based in metropolitan cities, with a high income level.

Step 3: Analyze Their Psychographics

Psychographics delve deeper into your ideal client's mind. It encompasses their lifestyle, values, attitudes, interests, and pain points. If we continue with the executive coaching example, your ideal clients may value continued personal development, struggle with work-life balance, and have an interest in leadership strategies.

Step 4: Identify Their Challenges and Goals

What problems or challenges does your ideal client face that your coaching services can solve? What goals do they aim to achieve? Understanding these will help you align your services with their needs, making your offerings more attractive to them.

Step 5: Determine Where They Spend Time

Knowing where your ideal clients spend their time, both online and offline, will guide your marketing and networking efforts. Are they active on certain social media platforms? Do they attend specific industry events or subscribe to certain publications?

Step 6: Fine-Tune Your Messaging

Once you've identified your ideal client, ensure that your messaging speaks directly to them. Your website, social media, and other marketing materials should all reflect an understanding of their needs, wants, and aspirations.

Remember, the process of identifying your ideal client is not a one-time task. As your coaching practice evolves, your ideal client may shift as well. Regularly revisiting and refining your ideal client profile can help keep your services and marketing efforts focused and effective, maximizing your client acquisition success.

Techniques for Attracting Potential Clients

Once you've identified your ideal client, the next step is to attract them to your coaching business.

Here are some proven techniques that can help you connect with potential clients and convince them of the value you offer.

Technique 1: Leverage Content Marketing

Content marketing is a powerful tool for attracting potential clients. By creating and sharing valuable content – such as blog posts, eBooks, podcasts, or videos – you can establish yourself as an expert in your coaching niche, providing solutions to the challenges your potential clients face. Ensure your content is SEO-optimized to increase your visibility on search engines.

Technique 2: Utilize Social Media

Social media platforms are a great way to reach your ideal clients. Share insightful content, engage with your followers, and showcase client testimonials to build trust and credibility. Additionally, platforms like LinkedIn and Facebook offer targeted advertising options that allow you to reach the exact demographics of your ideal client.

Technique 3: Offer Free Consultations or Webinars

Offering free consultations or webinars is an effective technique to showcase your coaching style and the value you can provide. It allows potential

clients to experience your services firsthand, making them more likely to engage with your business in the long term.

Technique 4: Build a Referral System

Happy clients can be your best ambassadors. Encourage your existing clients to refer others to your coaching services. You can incentivize this process by offering a discount or a free session for every successful referral.

Technique 5: Network Strategically

Networking, both online and offline, is a powerful way to expand your reach and connect with potential clients. Attend industry conferences, local meetups, or workshops to build in-person relationships. Join online forums, groups, or social media communities where your ideal clients gather. Genuine engagement often leads to valuable connections and referrals.

Technique 6: Collaborate with Complementary Businesses

Partnerships with businesses that offer complementary services can be beneficial. For instance, if you're a career coach, collaborating with recruitment agencies or educational institutions can provide access to a pool of potential clients.

Engaging with Your Potential Clients

Practice Active Listening

Active listening is essential in a coaching context. It involves fully concentrating, understanding, responding, and then remembering what your potential client is saying. This strategy ensures your clients feel heard, understood, and valued. In your initial interactions, be it over a call, email, or face-to-face meeting, focus on understanding your potential clients' needs and goals rather than selling your services.

Show Empathy

Empathy is the ability to understand and share the feelings of others. When potential clients approach you, they might be struggling with a problem they hope you can solve. Show understanding, care, and empathy towards their situation. This creates a bond of trust and makes them feel comfortable and safe.

Provide Personalized Insights

Once you understand your potential clients' needs, you can provide personalized insights or strategies. This not only shows your competence as a coach but also indicates that you're genuinely interested in their individual growth and success.

Be Responsive

Being responsive is a fundamental aspect of client engagement. Whenever potential clients reach out to you, respond promptly and professionally. This demonstrates that you respect their time and are serious about helping them.

Follow Up Regularly

Don't let potential clients forget about you after the first interaction. Follow up with them regularly, but make sure you're providing value in each interaction. You could share some helpful resources, offer a free mini-session, or provide valuable insights related to their situation.

Retaining Your Clients

Strategies for successful client retention:

Strategy 1: Deliver Consistent Value

At the heart of client retention is the value you provide. Ensure that your coaching services consistently help your clients achieve their goals. Regularly reassess and adjust your strategies to meet their evolving needs.

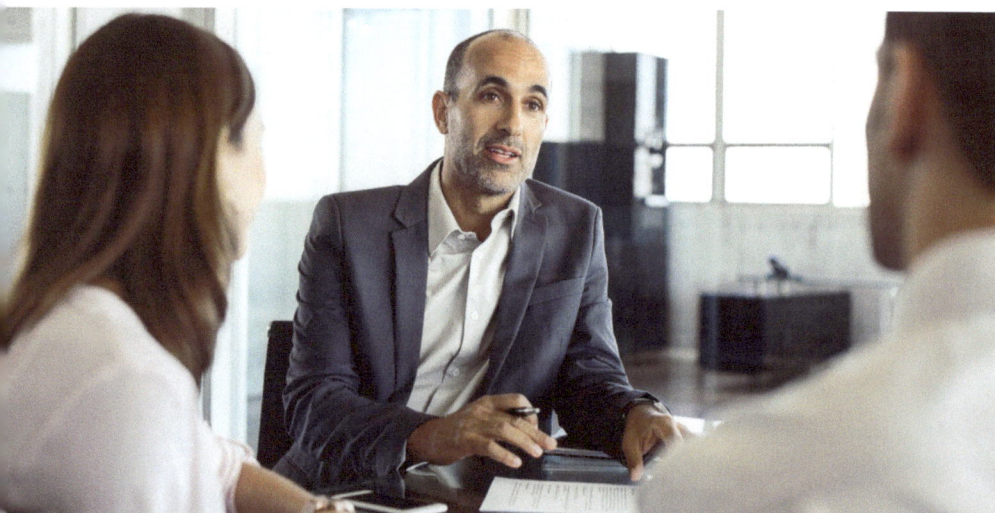

Strategy 2: Provide Exceptional Customer Service

Provide high-quality customer service to your clients. Be responsive to their inquiries, be flexible where possible, and always conduct yourself professionally. Remember, every interaction is an opportunity to reinforce their decision to choose you as their coach.

Strategy 3: Stay Connected

Keep the lines of communication open, even when a coaching session is not imminent. Regular check-ins, sharing relevant resources, or sending a newsletter are effective ways to stay connected and top of mind.

Strategy 4: Ask for Feedback

Solicit feedback from your clients about your services. Not only does this provide you with valuable insights on areas to improve, but it also makes your clients feel valued and involved in the process.

Strategy 5: Offer Loyalty Incentives

Consider implementing a loyalty program or offering incentives to long-term clients. This could be a discounted coaching package or exclusive access to new services. Such incentives show your appreciation and encourage continued business.

Strategy 6: Celebrate Client Successes

Celebrate your clients' milestones and successes, no matter how small. This makes them feel good about their progress and reinforces the value of your coaching.

FAQs

What is client acquisition in the context of a coaching business?

Client acquisition refers to the process of identifying, attracting, engaging, and converting potential clients into paying clients in a coaching business.

How do I identify my ideal client as a coach?

To identify your ideal client, consider your niche and expertise, and then define demographic characteristics, psychographics, challenges, goals, and behaviors that align with your coaching services.

What are some effective ways to attract potential coaching clients?

You can attract potential clients by creating valuable content, engaging actively on social media, hosting free webinars or consultations, encouraging client referrals, building strong professional networks, and partnering with businesses that offer complementary services to yours.

You've embarked on a journey through the pages of "Mastering the Art of Client Acquisition: A Guide for Coaches", exploring various facets of acquiring clients in the coaching business As you continue your journey in coaching, remember that client acquisition is not a one-time event but a continuous process.

The strategies and tips covered in this guide, when consistently applied, will equip you to steadily grow your client base, enhance your reputation, and achieve your career goals in coaching. Now, armed with knowledge and understanding, it's time to turn these insights into action. Master the art of client acquisition, and make your mark in the world of coaching.

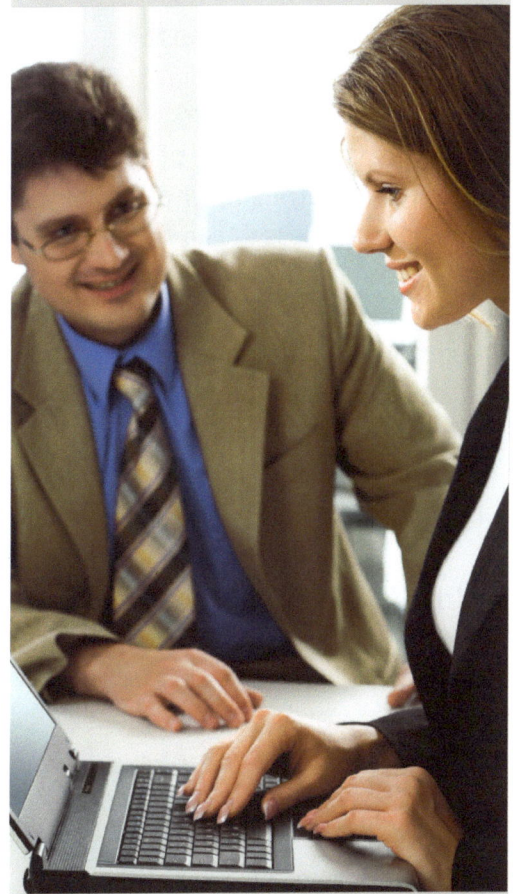

5 Key Metrics for Measuring Business Growth

As a business owner or entrepreneur, measuring your business growth is crucial for success. However, it can be challenging to determine which metrics to track and analyze. In this blog post, we'll dive into the 5 key metrics that are essential for measuring business growth. By understanding these metrics and their importance, you'll be able to make informed decisions and optimize your strategy for long-term success.

Revenue Growth: Key Metric for Measuring Business Success

Revenue growth is one of the most important metrics for measuring business success. It is a key indicator of how well a company is doing financially and can help identify areas for improvement. As a business owner or entrepreneur, understanding how to calculate and improve your revenue growth is crucial for long-term success.

What is Revenue Growth?

Revenue growth is the rate at which a company's revenue is increasing or decreasing over a certain period. This growth can be measured on a quarterly or yearly basis and is calculated by subtracting the previous period's revenue from the current period's revenue, dividing it by the previous period's revenue, and multiplying it by 100 to get a percentage.

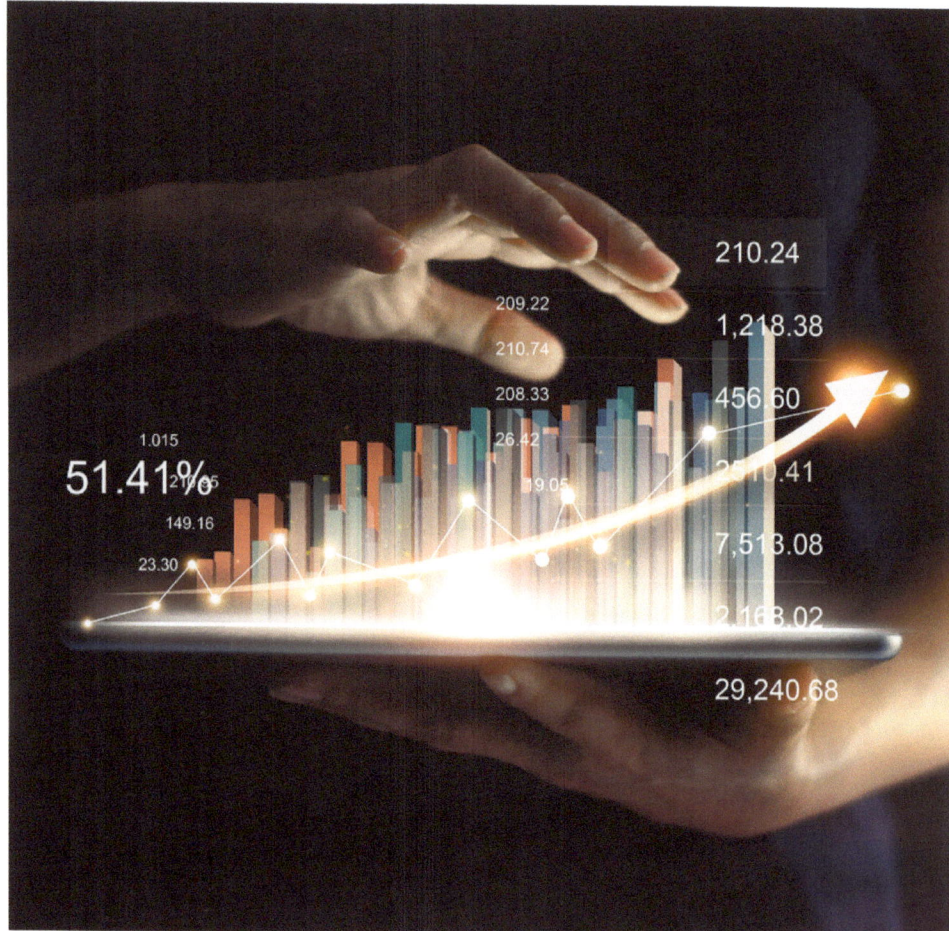

For example, if a company had $500,000 in revenue in the first quarter and $700,000 in the second quarter, the revenue growth rate for the second quarter would be ((700,000 - 500,000) / 500,000) * 100 = 40%.

Why is Revenue Growth Important?

Revenue growth is an essential metric for several reasons. Firstly, it shows how well a company is performing financially. If revenue is growing, it indicates that the company's products or services are in demand, and its operations are efficient. Secondly, revenue growth is a critical factor in determining a company's valuation. A company with strong revenue growth is typically more valuable than one with stagnant or declining revenue. Finally, revenue growth can help identify areas for improvement. By analyzing revenue growth over time, businesses can identify trends and make informed decisions about investments, marketing strategies, and new products or services.

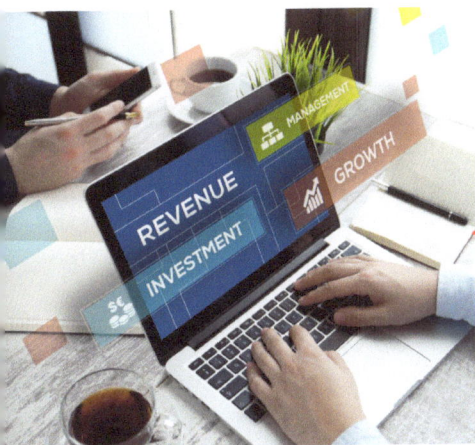

How to Improve Revenue Growth

Improving revenue growth can be challenging, but there are several strategies businesses can use to increase their revenue. One effective strategy is to expand the customer base. This can be achieved by investing in marketing campaigns to reach new audiences or by developing new products or services that appeal to a broader range of customers.

Another way to improve revenue growth is to increase the value of

each customer. This can be achieved by increasing the average order value, offering add-on products or services, or implementing a loyalty program to encourage repeat purchases.

Finally, reducing costs can help improve revenue growth. By identifying areas where costs can be reduced, businesses can increase their profit margins, which can lead to higher revenue growth.

Revenue growth is a crucial metric for measuring business success. It shows how well a company is performing financially, can help determine its valuation, and identify areas for improvement. By expanding the customer base, increasing the value of each customer, and reducing costs, businesses can improve their revenue growth and achieve long-term success. Regularly tracking and analyzing revenue growth is crucial for making informed decisions and optimizing business strategies for growth and success.

Customer Acquisition Cost (CAC)

For any business, acquiring new customers is essential for growth and success. However, it's also important to consider the cost of acquiring those customers. Customer Acquisition Cost (CAC)

is a key metric that measures the cost of acquiring each new customer. In this blog post, we'll explore what CAC is, why it matters, and how to calculate and improve it.

What is Customer Acquisition Cost (CAC)?

Customer Acquisition Cost (CAC) is the total cost a business incurs to acquire a new customer. This includes all marketing and advertising expenses, sales salaries and commissions, and any other costs associated with acquiring new customers. CAC is typically calculated by dividing the total cost of customer acquisition by the number of new customers acquired during a specific time period.

Why does CAC matter?

CAC is an essential metric for several reasons. Firstly, it helps businesses determine the return on investment (ROI) of their marketing and advertising campaigns. If the cost of acquiring a new customer is higher than the revenue generated by that customer, it indicates that the marketing campaign is not effective and needs to be adjusted.

Secondly, CAC is a critical factor in determining a company's profitability. If the cost of acquiring new customers is too high, it can eat into a company's profits and negatively impact its bottom line.

Finally, CAC can help identify areas for improvement in a business's sales and marketing processes. By analyzing CAC over time, businesses can identify trends and make informed decisions about where to invest their marketing and sales resources.

How to Calculate and Improve CAC

To calculate CAC, businesses need to track all expenses associated with customer acquisition, including marketing and advertising expenses, sales salaries and commissions, and any other costs. Once all costs have been identified, divide the total cost by the number of new customers acquired during a specific time period.

Improving CAC can be challenging, but there are several strategies businesses can use to reduce the cost of customer acquisition. One effective strategy is to target the right customers. By identifying the most profitable customer segments and focusing marketing and sales efforts on those segments, businesses can increase their ROI and reduce CAC.

Another way to improve CAC is

is to improve the efficiency of the sales and marketing processes. This can be achieved by investing in automation tools, streamlining the sales process, and ensuring that marketing efforts are targeted and effective.

Finally, businesses can improve CAC by reducing the time it takes to close a sale. By shortening the sales cycle and increasing conversion rates, businesses can reduce the cost of customer acquisition and increase their profitability.

Customer Acquisition Cost (CAC) is an essential metric for any business that wants to achieve long-term success. By tracking and analyzing CAC, businesses can determine the ROI of their marketing and advertising campaigns, identify areas for improvement in their sales and marketing processes, and increase their profitability.

By targeting the right customers, improving the efficiency of the sales and marketing processes, and reducing the time it takes to close a sale, businesses can improve their CAC and achieve their growth and success goals.

Customer Retention Rate

As a business owner or entrepreneur, acquiring new customers is crucial for growth and success. However, it's equally important to retain existing customers. Customer retention rate is a key metric that measures the percentage of customers who continue to do business with a company over time. In this blog post, we'll explore what customer retention rate is, why it matters, and how to calculate and improve it.

What is Customer Retention Rate?

Customer retention rate is the percentage of customers who continue to do business with a company over a certain period. This period can be a month, a quarter, or a year. Customer retention rate is typically calculated by dividing the number of customers who continue to do business with a company over a specific period by the total number of customers at the beginning of that period.

Why does Customer Retention Rate matter?

Customer retention rate is an essential metric for several reasons. Firstly, it shows how well a company is retaining its customers. A high customer retention rate indicates that customers are satisfied with a company's products or services, and are likely to continue doing business with that company in the future. Secondly, customer retention rate is a critical factor in determining a company's profitability. It costs more to acquire new customers than it does to retain existing ones, so a high customer retention rate can lead to increased profitability. Finally, customer retention rate can help identify areas for improvement in a business's operations. By analyzing customer retention rate over time, businesses can identify trends and make informed decisions about how to improve their products or services and customer experience.

How to Calculate and Improve Customer Retention Rate

To calculate customer retention rate, businesses need to track the number of customers who continue to do business with them over a specific period. Once this number is determined, divide it by the total number of customers at the beginning of that period.

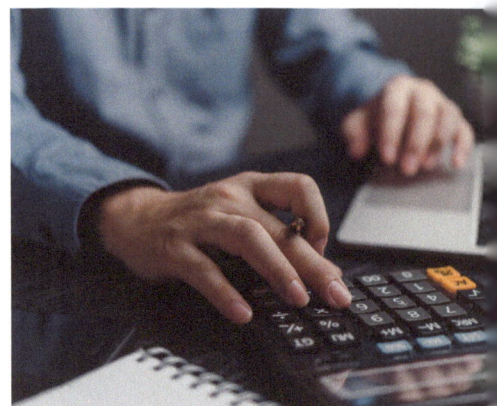

Improving customer retention rate can be challenging, but there are several strategies businesses can use to increase customer loyalty and retention. One effective strategy is to provide exceptional customer service. This can be achieved by responding to customer inquiries and complaints promptly, offering personalized service, and going above and beyond to meet customer needs.

Another way to improve customer retention rate is to offer loyalty programs and incentives. This can include offering discounts or rewards for repeat purchases, providing exclusive content or services, or creating a VIP program for long-term customers.

Finally, businesses can improve customer retention rate by consistently delivering high-quality products or services. By focusing on product or service excellence, businesses can create a loyal customer base that is more likely to continue doing business with them over time.

Customer retention rate is an essential metric for any business that wants to achieve long-term success. By tracking and analyzing customer retention rate, businesses can determine how well they are retaining their customers, identify areas for improvement, and increase their profitability. By providing exceptional customer service, offering loyalty programs and incentives, and consistently delivering high-quality products or services, businesses can improve their customer retention rate and achieve their growth and success goals.

Net Promoter Score (NPS)

As a business owner or entrepreneur, understanding how your customers perceive your business is crucial for growth and success. Net Promoter Score (NPS) is a key metric that measures customer loyalty and satisfaction. In this blog post, we'll explore what NPS is, why it matters, and how to calculate and improve it.

What is Net Promoter Score (NPS)?

Net Promoter Score (NPS) is a metric that measures customer loyalty and satisfaction. It asks customers how likely they are to recommend a company to a friend or colleague on a scale of 0 to 10. Customers who respond with a score of 9 or 10 are considered "promoters" of the company, while those who respond with a score of 0 to 6 are considered "detractors." The NPS score is calculated by subtracting the percentage of detractors from the percentage of promoters.

Why does Net Promoter Score (NPS) matter?

Net Promoter Score (NPS) is an essential metric for several reasons. Firstly, it shows how likely customers are to recommend a company to others. Word-of-mouth recommendations are a powerful marketing tool, and a high NPS score indicates that customers

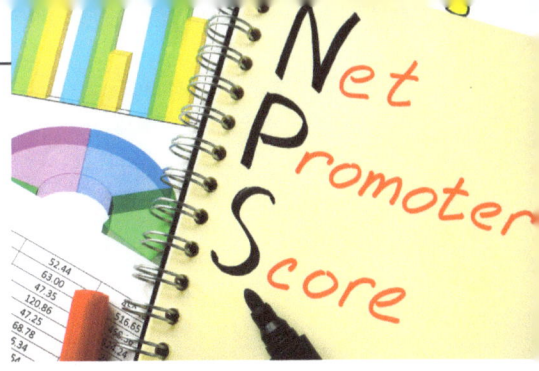

are satisfied with a company's products or services and are likely to promote them to others.

Secondly, NPS is a critical factor in determining a company's customer satisfaction levels. By measuring how likely customers are to recommend a company, businesses can identify areas for improvement in their products or services and customer experience.

Finally, NPS can help identify areas for improvement in a business's operations. By analyzing NPS over time, businesses can identify trends and make informed decisions about how to improve their products or services and customer experience.

How to Calculate and Improve Net Promoter Score (NPS)

To calculate NPS, businesses need to ask their customers how likely they are to recommend their products or services to others on a scale of 0 to 10. Once this data is collected, the percentage of promoters and detractors can be determined, and the NPS score can be calculated by subtracting the percentage of detractors from the percentage of promoters.

Improving NPS can be challenging, but there are several strategies businesses can use to increase customer loyalty and satisfaction. One effective strategy is to provide exceptional customer service. This can be achieved by responding to customer inquiries and complaints promptly, offering personalized service, and going above and beyond to meet customer needs.

Another way to improve NPS is to focus on product or service excellence. By consistently delivering high-quality products or services, businesses can create a loyal customer base that is more likely to recommend them to others.

Finally, businesses can improve NPS by asking for customer feedback and acting on it. By listening to customer concerns and suggestions, businesses can identify areas for improvement and make changes to improve the customer experience.

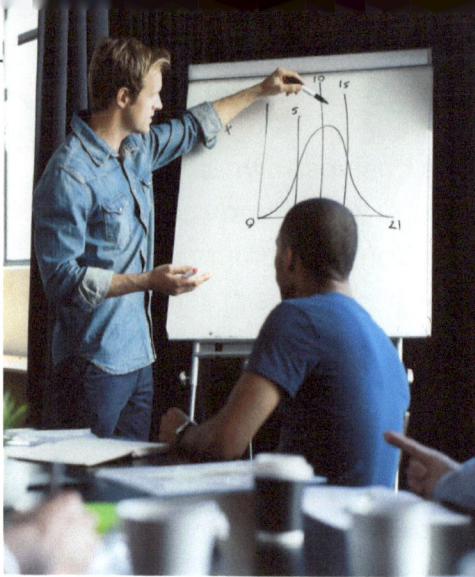

Gross Profit Margin: A Key Metric for Financial Health

Gross profit margin is a key metric that measures a company's financial health. It's an essential metric for any business, as it shows the percentage of revenue left after accounting for the cost of goods sold (COGS).

What is Gross Profit Margin?

Gross profit margin is the percentage of revenue left after accounting for the cost of goods sold (COGS). It's calculated by subtracting COGS from revenue and dividing the result by revenue, then multiplying it by 100 to get a percentage.

Why does Gross Profit Margin matter?

Gross profit margin is an essential metric for several reasons. Firstly, it shows the percentage of revenue that a company has left after

accounting for COGS. This metric is important because it indicates how efficiently a company is operating. If gross profit margin is high, it indicates that a company is generating revenue and keeping costs under control. On the other hand, if gross profit margin is low, it may indicate that a company needs to re-evaluate its pricing strategy or reduce costs.

Secondly, gross profit margin is a critical factor in determining a company's profitability. A higher gross profit margin means that a company has more revenue available to cover its operating expenses and invest in growth. On the other hand, a lower gross profit margin means that a company has less revenue available to cover its expenses and may struggle to grow or remain profitable.

Finally, gross profit margin can help identify areas for improvement in a business's operations. By analyzing gross profit margin over time, businesses can identify trends and make informed decisions about how to improve their products or services and reduce costs.

How to Calculate and Improve Gross Profit Margin

To calculate gross profit margin, businesses need to subtract COGS from revenue, divide the result by revenue, and multiply by 100 to get a percentage.

Improving gross profit margin can be challenging, but there are several strategies businesses can use to increase their gross profit margin.

One effective strategy is to increase prices. By increasing prices, businesses can increase revenue and improve their gross profit margin. However, businesses need to be careful not to price themselves out of the market or lose customers to competitors.

Another way to improve gross profit margin is to reduce the cost of goods sold (COGS). This can be achieved by negotiating better prices with suppliers, optimizing the supply chain, or using more efficient manufacturing processes.

Finally, businesses can improve gross profit margin by increasing sales volume. By increasing sales volume, businesses can spread their fixed costs over more units, which can help improve their gross profit margin.

Measuring business growth is a continuous process that requires consistent monitoring and analysis of key metrics. By focusing on revenue growth, customer acquisition cost, customer retention rate, net promoter score, and gross profit margin, you'll have a comprehensive understanding of your business's health and can make informed decisions for its growth and success. Remember to regularly track and analyze these metrics to optimize your strategy and achieve your business goals.

Customer-Centric Marketing: Building Loyalty and Sales

As businesses continue to adapt to changing consumer expectations and technological advancements, there has been a significant shift toward more customer-focused strategies. This evolution has led to the rise of Customer-Centric Marketing, an approach that moves beyond traditional methods to deliver highly personalized and meaningful experiences. At its core, customer-centric marketing is about understanding and addressing the needs, preferences, and motivations of customers, positioning them not simply as buyers but as active participants in the brand journey.

Understanding Customer-Centric Marketing

Definition and Principles

Customer-Centric Marketing is a strategy that places the customer at the center of marketing design and delivery. It's about understanding the needs, preferences, and behaviors of customers and creating marketing strategies that provide value and enhance their experience. This approach contrasts with traditional product-centric marketing, which focuses primarily on promoting products or services.

The core principles of customer-centric marketing include:

Empathy: Understanding customer emotions, needs, and expectations.

Personalization: Tailoring marketing efforts to individual customer preferences.

Consistency: Ensuring a cohesive customer experience across all touchpoints.

Responsiveness: Adapting quickly to customer feedback and market changes.

Value-driven: Focusing on delivering genuine value to customers, not just selling a product.

Evolution in the Digital Age

The digital age has transformed customer-centric marketing. With the advent of advanced

FROGMAN MINDFULNESS

Jon Macaskill
US Navy SEAL Commander (Ret)
Keynote Speaking
One on One Coaching
Mindfulness Teaching
www.frogmanmindfulness.com
757-619-1211

analytics, social media, and mobile technology, businesses can now access deeper insights into customer behaviors and preferences. This evolution has led to more personalized and targeted marketing strategies.

Digital platforms have also enabled two-way communication, allowing customers to interact with brands more directly and personally. This interaction has shifted the power balance, with customers now having a louder voice and higher expectations regarding their experiences with brands.

Importance of Understanding Customer Behavior

Understanding customer behavior is pivotal in customer-centric marketing. It involves analyzing how customers interact with your brand, what drives their purchasing decisions, and what their pain points are. This understanding can come from various data sources, such as purchase history, social media activity, and customer feedback.

By comprehensively understanding customer behavior, businesses can:

Predict Future Needs: Anticipate what customers will want or need next.

Customize Marketing Messages: Tailor marketing communications to resonate more effectively with different customer segments.

Improve Customer Experience: Identify and address pain points to enhance the overall customer journey.

Build Stronger Relationships: Foster loyalty by showing customers that their preferences and feedback are valued and acted upon.

Developing a Customer-Centric Strategy

In the realm of customer-centric marketing, developing a strategy that effectively resonates with and engages your target audience is crucial. This section outlines the key steps and considerations in crafting a customer-centric marketing strategy.

Steps to Create a Customer-Centric Marketing Strategy

Understand Your Customer

Conduct thorough market research to understand your customer demographics, preferences, pain points, and buying behaviors.

Utilize customer feedback, surveys, social media listening, and data analytics to gain deeper insights.

Segment Your Audience

Segmenting your customer base involves grouping individuals by shared traits such as age, purchasing habits, interests, or geographic location. This targeted approach allows you to craft messages, offers, and experiences that resonate more deeply with each group. By tailoring your marketing to the unique needs of each segment, you improve engagement, relevance, and overall campaign effectiveness.

data to refine your approach and stay aligned with customer expectations.

Create Personalized Experiences

Design marketing campaigns and customer experiences that are personalized and relevant to each customer segment.

Utilize personalization technology and data-driven insights to tailor content, offers, and communications.

Integrate Across Channels

Ensure a consistent and seamless customer experience across all channels, including digital, in-store, and customer service.

Align messaging, branding, and customer interactions across all touchpoints.

Foster a Customer-Centric Culture

Fostering a company-wide commitment to customer-centricity begins with ensuring that every team member recognizes the value of putting the customer first. This cultural shift involves clear communication, leadership support, and alignment across departments. Equipping employees with ongoing training, practical tools, and relevant resources empowers them to consistently deliver exceptional service and build meaningful connections with customers at every touchpoint.

Define Customer Journeys

Map out the customer journey for each segment, from awareness to purchase and beyond.

Identify key touchpoints and opportunities for engagement throughout the journey.

Develop a Value Proposition

Craft a compelling value proposition that clearly communicates the unique benefits your brand offers to the customer.

Ensure that this proposition resonates with your target segments and addresses their specific needs and desires.

Leverage Data and Insights

Use customer data and insights to inform your strategy and decision-making process.

Continually gather and analyze

Integration of Customer Data and Insights

Incorporating customer data and insights into your strategy is non-negotiable. This data should inform every aspect of your marketing, from campaign design to product development. It's crucial to have systems in place that can collect, analyze, and leverage customer data effectively. This includes using CRM systems, analytics tools, and customer feedback mechanisms.

Customization and Personalization Techniques

The heart of a customer-centric strategy lies in customization and personalization. This can range from personalized emails and targeted advertising to customized products or services. Advances in technology, like AI and machine learning, are making it easier to personalize at scale, providing customers with experiences that feel uniquely tailored to them.

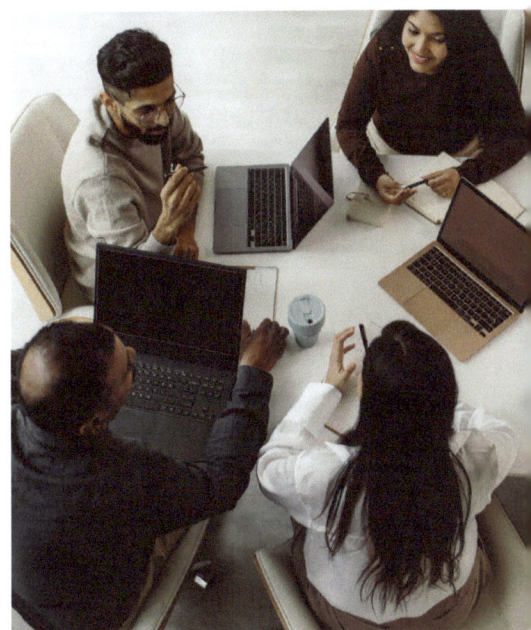

Tools and Technologies for Customer-Centric Marketing

The successful implementation of a customer-centric marketing strategy heavily relies on leveraging the right tools and technologies. These enable businesses to gather insights, personalize experiences, and engage with customers more effectively. This section outlines key tools and technologies essential for customer-centric marketing.

CRM Systems

CRM systems are foundational in managing customer data and interactions.

They help in tracking customer interactions, managing leads, and personalizing customer experiences.

Popular CRM platforms include Salesforce, HubSpot, and Zoho CRM, each offering unique features tailored to different business needs.

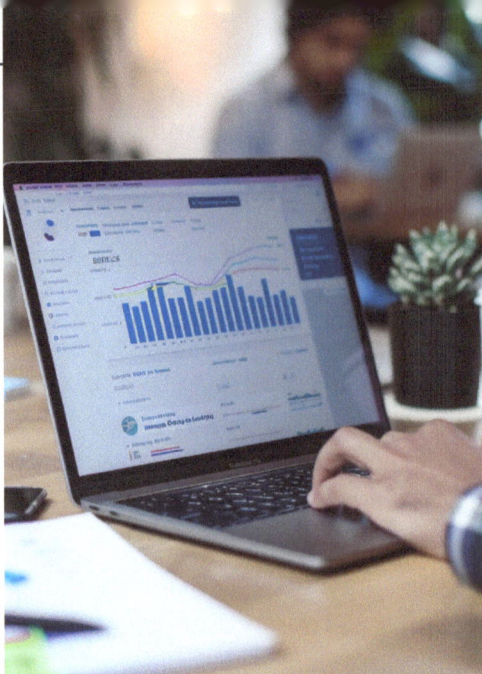

Data Analytics Tools

Analytics tools provide valuable insights into customer behavior, preferences, and trends.

They enable marketers to make data-driven decisions and tailor strategies accordingly.

Tools like Google Analytics, Adobe Analytics, and Tableau offer in-depth analysis of web traffic, customer engagement, and conversion metrics.

Digital Marketing Platforms

These platforms streamline and automate marketing processes like email campaigns, social media posting, and lead nurturing.

Automation tools can personalize content delivery based on customer data, improving engagement and efficiency.

Examples include Marketo, Mailchimp, and Hootsuite, each offering different automation capabilities.

Social Media Management Tools

Social media tools help manage multiple platforms, schedule posts, and engage with audiences efficiently.

Listening tools track brand mentions, customer sentiments, and trends across social platforms.

Sprout Social, Buffer, and Brandwatch are examples of tools that offer comprehensive social media management and analytics.

Personalization and Engagement Technologies

These technologies include AI-driven recommendation engines and chatbots.

They enhance customer experience through personalized product recommendations, tailored content, and instant customer support.

Platforms like Algolia for search personalization and Drift for conversational marketing are increasingly popular.

Customer Feedback Tools

Gathering and analyzing customer feedback is vital for understanding customer satisfaction and areas for improvement.

Tools like SurveyMonkey, Qualtrics, and Net Promoter Score (NPS) surveys provide platforms for collecting and analyzing customer feedback.

Mobile Marketing Tools

With the increasing use of smartphones, mobile marketing tools are essential for engaging customers on mobile devices.

These tools include mobile app analytics, SMS marketing platforms, and mobile-friendly email marketing software.

Integrating Technology for Enhanced Engagement

Integrating these technologies allows for a more holistic view of the customer and enables more effective engagement strategies. It's important to choose tools that not only meet the specific needs of your business but also integrate well with each other for a seamless flow of data and insights.

Building Customer Loyalty and Trust

Building customer loyalty and trust is a crucial aspect of customer-centric marketing. This section explores strategies and techniques for nurturing long-term relationships with customers, which are vital for sustained business growth and success.

Techniques for Nurturing Customer Relationships

Provide Exceptional Customer Service

Exceptional customer service is the cornerstone of customer loyalty. It involves being responsive, empathetic, and proactive in addressing customer needs and concerns.

Implementing customer service best practices, such as quick response times, personalized support, and effective problem-solving, can significantly enhance customer satisfaction.

Deliver Consistent Quality and Value

Consistency in product or service quality assures customers of reliability, encouraging repeat business.

Continuously strive to offer value through your products or services, which goes beyond just meeting basic expectations to truly delighting customers.

Engage Regularly and Meaningfully

Maintaining regular engagement with customers through personalized messages, loyalty programs, and active social media presence helps keep your brand visible and relevant. Meaningful engagement goes a step further by aligning your communication with each customer's interests, habits, and preferences. This thoughtful approach fosters stronger connections, builds trust, and encourages continued loyalty over time.

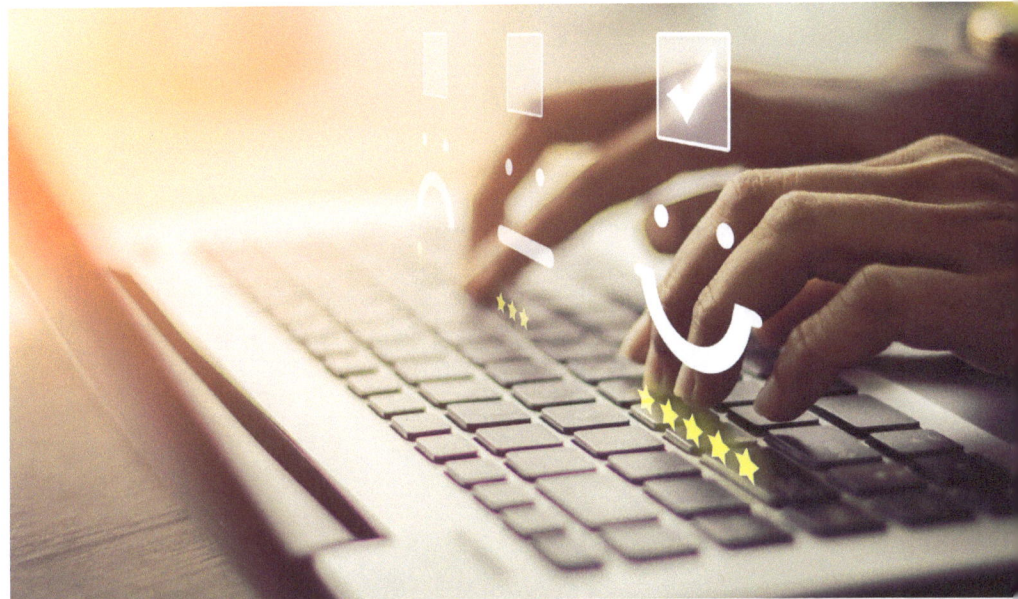

Foster a Community Around Your Brand

Building a community, either online or offline, where customers can interact, share experiences, and feel a sense of belonging can deepen their emotional connection to the brand.

Implement Loyalty Programs

Loyalty programs that reward repeat purchases or engagement can significantly boost customer retention.

These programs should be easy to understand and genuinely beneficial, offering discounts, exclusive access, or other perks.

Role of Content Marketing and Social Media

Utilize Content Marketing

Content marketing can be a powerful tool for building trust and loyalty. By providing valuable, relevant content that educates, entertains, or informs, you position your brand as a helpful and knowledgeable industry leader.

Blogs, videos, webinars, and e-books are various formats that can be used to engage customers and keep them interested in your brand.

Leverage Social Media Platforms

Social media platforms offer a great avenue to connect with customers, share content, and respond to queries and feedback.

Regular, authentic, and interactive posts can help in maintaining an active and positive presence, fostering trust and loyalty.

Strategies for Handling Feedback and Complaints

Encourage and Act on Customer Feedback

Encourage customers to share their feedback and make it easy for them to do so through surveys, reviews, and social media channels.

Actively listening and responding to feedback, both positive and negative, demonstrates that you value customer opinions and are committed to continuous improvement.

Effectively Manage Complaints

Handling complaints effectively is critical in maintaining customer trust. This includes acknowledging the issue, offering a sincere apology, and providing a timely and satisfactory resolution.

Turning a negative experience into a positive one can often result in even stronger customer loyalty.

Measuring Success and Adapting Strategies

To ensure the effectiveness of customer-centric marketing, it's crucial to measure success and continually adapt strategies based on insights and market dynamics. This section discusses key performance indicators (KPIs), the role of feedback and market research, and future trends in adapting customer-centric marketing strategies.

Key Performance Indicators (KPIs) for Customer-Centric Marketing

Customer Satisfaction Score (CSAT)

Customer Satisfaction Score (CSAT) is a key metric used to assess how satisfied customers are with a specific product, service, or interaction. It is commonly measured through short surveys where customers rate their experience on a numerical scale, offering immediate feedback.

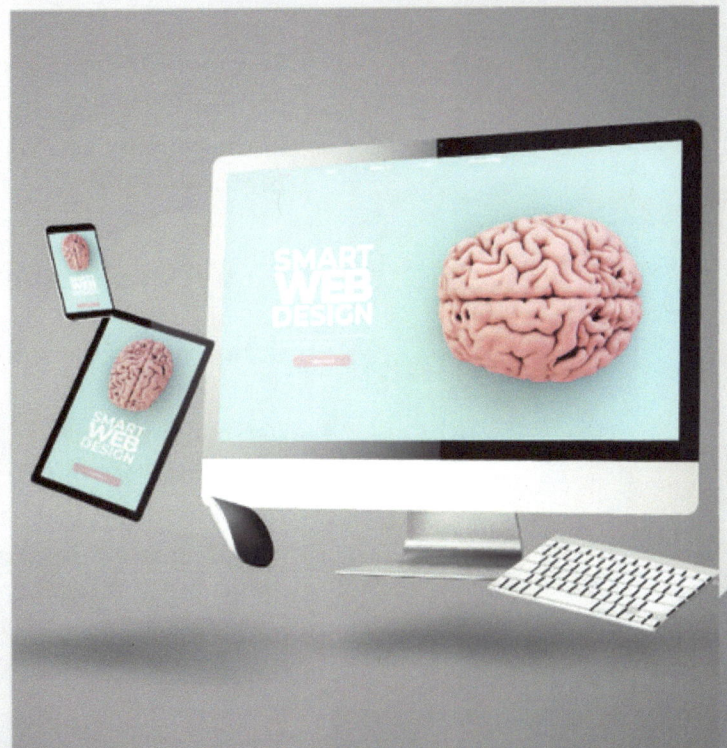

Net Promoter Score (NPS)

NPS assesses customer loyalty by asking how likely customers are to recommend your brand to others. It's a strong indicator of customer satisfaction and loyalty.

Customer Lifetime Value (CLV)

CLV predicts the total value a business can expect from a single customer account. It helps in understanding the long-term value of maintaining customer relationships.

Customer Retention Rate

This metric measures how well a business retains its customers over a period. High retention rates are often indicative of successful customer-centric strategies.

Conversion Rates

Conversion rates, especially in the context of targeted marketing campaigns, can indicate the effectiveness of personalization and engagement strategies.

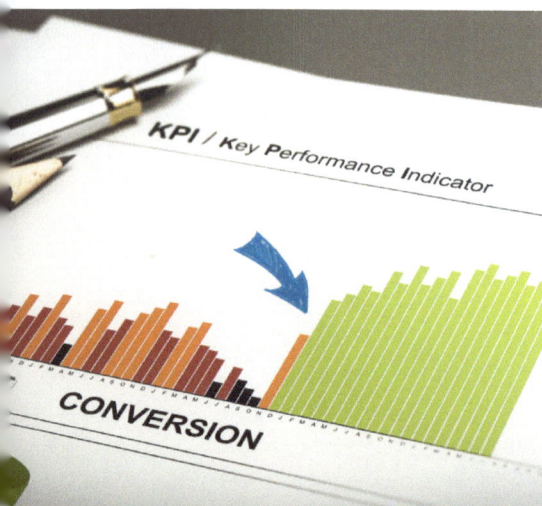

Social Media Engagement

Metrics such as likes, shares, comments, and brand mentions on social media provide insights into brand popularity and customer engagement.

Role of Feedback and Market Research

Continuous Customer Feedback

Regularly collecting and analyzing customer feedback is vital for understanding their needs and how well they are being met.

Feedback can be gathered through surveys, social media listening, customer reviews, and direct customer interactions.

Market Research

Keeping abreast of market trends and consumer behavior patterns through ongoing market research is crucial for adapting and refining strategies.

This includes studying competitors, industry trends, and emerging customer preferences.

Strategy Adaptation

Data-Driven Decision Making

Use insights from key performance indicators, customer feedback, and market research to guide smarter decisions in both marketing initiatives and product innovation.

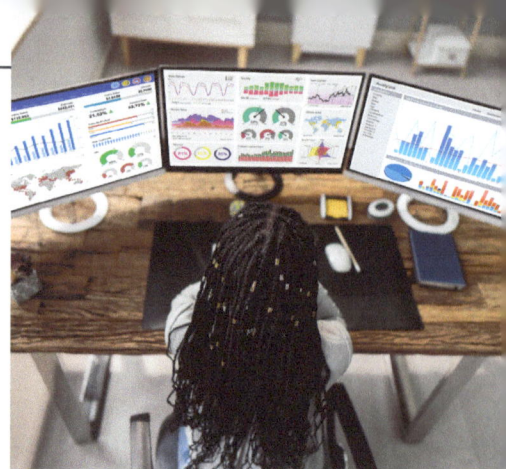

Agility and Flexibility

The ability to quickly adapt to changing customer needs and market conditions is a key aspect of a successful customer-centric approach.

This may involve pivoting strategies, exploring new marketing channels, or innovating product offerings.

Innovation Based on Trends and Customer Insights

Stay ahead of industry trends and leverage new technologies to enhance customer experience and engagement.

Innovate based on customer insights to meet evolving needs and stay competitive.

Looking Towards the Future

Stay informed about emerging trends and technologies that could impact customer behavior and expectations.

This proactive approach enables businesses to adapt their strategies ahead of time, maintaining relevance and competitiveness.

Embracing customer-centric marketing is essential for businesses that want to remain relevant and competitive. It goes far beyond promoting products or services. At its core, this approach is about creating meaningful connections with customers by truly understanding their needs, preferences, and behaviors. Companies that adopt a customer-first mindset focus on delivering value at every stage of the customer journey. This means using the right tools, data, and strategies to personalize experiences, solve real problems, and anticipate future expectations. Customer-centric marketing requires a commitment to listening, learning, and evolving based on customer feedback and market trends. Success is no longer measured solely by short-term sales but also by customer retention, loyalty, and the ability to turn satisfied customers into brand advocates. When done well, customer-centric marketing builds trust, encourages repeat business, and strengthens a company's reputation. It is a powerful path toward long-term, sustainable growth in a customer-driven world.

Strategies for Enhancing Customer Lifetime Value

Understanding and maximizing Customer Lifetime Value (CLV) has become a strategic priority for businesses aiming to build long-lasting customer relationships and drive sustainable growth. CLV measures the total revenue a customer is expected to generate over the entire span of their relationship with a company. This metric goes beyond individual transactions, encouraging brands to see the bigger picture—how each interaction contributes to overall profitability. A higher CLV often translates to better customer retention, increased brand loyalty, and more predictable revenue streams.

Focusing on CLV allows businesses to allocate resources more effectively. Rather than spending heavily on constantly acquiring new customers, companies can invest in deepening relationships with existing ones. Personalized marketing, exceptional customer service, loyalty programs, and continuous engagement all play a vital role in increasing CLV. These efforts not only increase the value of each customer but also create advocates who bring in additional customers through word-of-mouth and referrals.

Building a strategy around CLV requires understanding customer behavior, anticipating future needs, and delivering consistent value. Businesses that prioritize customer satisfaction and experience tend to see longer retention periods and higher average purchase values. By analyzing CLV, companies can identify which customer segments are most profitable and tailor their offerings accordingly. This focus on long-term value helps create a more stable and resilient business model, where customer loyalty becomes a key driver of growth and success.

Understanding Your Customers

Deep Customer Analysis

At the heart of enhancing Customer Lifetime Value (CLV) lies a profound understanding of your customers. It's more than just knowing who they are; it's about understanding their interactions with your brand, their purchasing habits, and what drives their loyalty. To achieve this, businesses need to dive into deep customer analysis. Utilizing data analytics tools can provide invaluable insights into customer behaviors, preferences, and needs. This process involves studying their purchase history, browsing patterns, and engagement metrics. Such data-driven insights help in comprehending the underlying motivations of customers and tailoring products and services to meet their specific needs and desires.

Segmentation and Personalization

Segmentation is another vital aspect of understanding your customers. By categorizing customers into distinct groups based on their value, behaviors, and preferences, businesses can develop more targeted and effective strategies. This personalization extends to marketing efforts, product development, and customer service approaches. For instance, high-value customers might receive more personalized services or exclusive offers, which not only enhances their experience but also encourages further engagement and loyalty.

Customer Feedback and Continuous Learning

Engaging with customers to gather feedback is crucial. This can be achieved through various means such as surveys, focus groups, or direct interactions. Feedback provides a direct line into the customer's perspective, offering businesses a clear view of what's working and what isn't. Moreover, it's not just about collecting feedback but also acting on it. This shows customers that their opinions are valued and considered, fostering a stronger relationship.

Empathy and Understanding

Lastly, understanding your customers also means empathizing with them. It's about putting yourself in their shoes and viewing your products and services from their perspective. This empathetic approach can reveal gaps in customer experience and opportunities for improvement. It also builds a more human and relatable brand image, which is essential in today's market where customers are increasingly seeking authentic and personalized experiences.

Improving Product and Service Quality

Emphasizing Quality in Offerings

Quality is a pivotal aspect that drives customer satisfaction and loyalty, directly impacting Customer Lifetime Value (CLV). Businesses must prioritize the quality of their products and services to ensure they not only meet but exceed customer expectations. This commitment to quality involves a continuous process of evaluation and improvement. Regular assessments of your offerings can help identify areas that need enhancement, ensuring your products and services stay relevant and appealing to your customer base.

Incorporating Customer Feedback

An effective way to improve quality is through active customer feedback mechanisms. Encourage your customers to share their opinions and experiences with your products or services. This feedback is a goldmine of insights, revealing what customers appreciate and what areas might need refinement. More importantly, acting on this feedback demonstrates to customers that their opinions are valued and considered, fostering a deeper sense of loyalty and trust in your brand.

Consistent Quality Assurance

Maintaining consistency in quality is key. Implementing stringent quality control processes ensures that every product or service offered meets a high standard. This consistency is crucial for building customer trust and satisfaction, as customers are more likely to return and recommend your brand when they can rely on the quality of your offerings.

Innovation and Continuous Improvement

Staying ahead in the market often requires innovation and adaptation. Investing in research and development can lead to improvements in your products and services, addressing evolving customer needs and preferences. This proactive approach not only enhances the quality of your offerings but also positions your brand as a forward-thinking leader in your industry.

Exceeding Expectations

Finally, aim to exceed customer expectations. This could mean adding unique features to your products, offering exceptional customer service, or providing personalized experiences that delight your customers. By going above and beyond what is expected, your business can create memorable experiences that resonate with customers, encouraging them to return and advocate for your brand.

Personalizing Customer Experience

Tailoring Experiences to Individual Needs

Personalizing the customer experience is a crucial strategy in enhancing Customer Lifetime Value (CLV). t's about moving beyond a one-size-fits-all approach and tailoring interactions and offerings to meet the individual needs and preferences of each customer. This personalization can be achieved through the use of customer data, which provides insights into their past interactions, preferences, and purchasing habits. By leveraging this data, businesses can create highly targeted and relevant experiences that resonate deeply with each customer.

Customizing Communications and Offers

Effective personalization also extends to how businesses communicate with their customers. Customized communications, whether through email, social media, or direct mail, should reflect the customer's previous interactions with the brand and their personal preferences. This can include personalized product recommendations, tailored promotions, or content that aligns with their interests. Similarly, customized offers, such as special discounts or exclusive access to new products, can be highly effective in enhancing engagement and loyalty.

Leveraging Technology for Personalization

Advancements in technology have made it easier to personalize customer experiences at scale. Tools like Customer Relationship Management (CRM) systems, AI, and machine learning algorithms can analyze large sets of customer data and automate personalized interactions. This technology can help predict customer needs and preferences, allowing businesses to proactively offer solutions and experiences that are more likely to be well-received.

The Human Touch

While technology plays a crucial role in personalization, the human element remains vital. Personal interactions, empathy, and understanding the customer's perspective are irreplaceable aspects of personalizing the customer experience. Training staff to recognize and respond to individual customer needs and

preferences can significantly enhance the personal touch, making customers feel truly valued and understood.

Fostering Customer Loyalty

Building Strong Customer Relationships

Fostering customer loyalty is fundamental in enhancing Customer Lifetime Value (CLV). It's about creating strong, lasting relationships with customers that go beyond transactional interactions. This involves understanding their needs, providing exceptional service, and consistently delivering value. Loyal customers are more likely to make repeat purchases, try new offerings, and recommend your brand to others.

Developing Loyalty Programs

One effective strategy for fostering loyalty is through well-designed loyalty programs. These programs can reward customers for their repeated business, encouraging them to continue choosing your brand. Rewards can vary from points, discounts, special offers, or

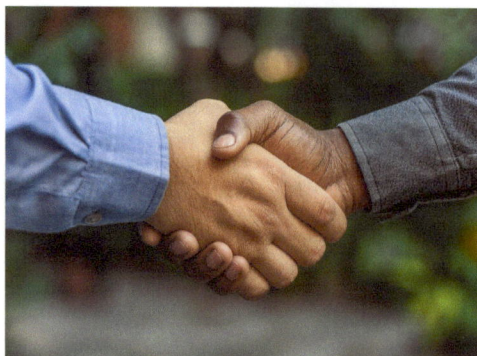

exclusive access to new products. The key is to make the rewards appealing and relevant to your customers, providing them with a tangible incentive to remain loyal.

Providing Exceptional Customer Service

Exceptional customer service is at the heart of customer loyalty. This means not only addressing customer issues promptly and efficiently but also going the

extra mile to exceed their expectations. Training your staff to be attentive, responsive, and empathetic to customer needs plays a crucial role. Personalized service, where customers feel heard and valued, can significantly impact their loyalty to your brand.

Engaging with Customers Consistently

Consistent engagement is vital in maintaining customer loyalty. This can be achieved through regular communication, such as newsletters, personalized emails, or social media interactions. Keeping customers informed about new products, offers, and company news keeps your brand top-of-mind. Furthermore, engaging customers in feedback and involving them in the development of new products or services can make them feel like a valued part of your business.

Creating a Community Around Your Brand

Building a community around your brand can further deepen customer loyalty. This can involve creating online forums, social media groups, or hosting events where customers can interact with each other and your brand. A sense of community can foster a stronger emotional connection with your brand, making customers more loyal and engaged.

Maximizing Customer Engagement

Creating Engaging Touchpoints

Maximizing customer engagement plays a crucial role in boosting Customer Lifetime Value (CLV). It involves designing meaningful, consistent, and interactive touchpoints that connect with customers emotionally and intellectually throughout their entire journey with your brand. True engagement means fostering interest, encouraging two-way communication, delivering personalized experiences, and building trust that transforms occasional buyers into loyal, long-term advocates.

Utilizing Content Marketing

Content marketing is a powerful tool in this endeavor. By producing valuable, relevant, and engaging content, businesses can attract and retain customer attention. This content can range from informative blog posts, engaging videos, informative podcasts, to interactive social media posts. The key is to provide content that adds value to your customers, whether it's through entertainment, education, or inspiration, thereby fostering a deeper connection with your brand.

Leveraging Social Media Platforms

Social media platforms are invaluable for customer engagement. They provide a space for businesses to interact with customers in real-time, respond to their queries, and engage in conversations.

Regularly posting updates, running interactive campaigns, and responding to customer comments and messages can significantly enhance engagement. Additionally, social media analytics can offer insights into customer preferences and behaviors, allowing for more targeted and effective engagement strategies.

Personalized Customer Experiences

Personalization plays a crucial role in engagement. Tailoring customer experiences based on individual preferences and past interactions can make customers feel valued and understood. This can be achieved through personalized email marketing, product recommendations, and customized offers. The more relevant the experience is to the customer, the more likely they are to engage with your brand.

Encouraging Customer Participation

Engaging customers also means encouraging their participation. This can be through customer reviews, testimonials, or user-generated content. Inviting customers to share their experiences or participate in brand-related activities creates a sense of ownership and community. It also provides valuable content that can attract new customers.

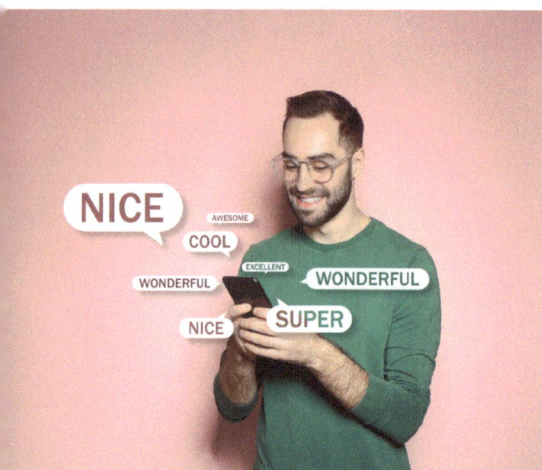

Leveraging Technology for Enhanced Interactions

Integrating Advanced Technologies

In the digital age, leveraging technology is key to enhancing customer interactions and, consequently, Customer Lifetime Value (CLV). Technology can facilitate more efficient, personalized, and engaging interactions with customers. By integrating advanced technological solutions, businesses can streamline processes, gain deeper insights into customer behavior, and

deliver a more satisfying customer experience.

Utilizing Customer Relationship Management (CRM) Systems

One of the most effective tools for enhancing customer interactions is a Customer Relationship Management (CRM) system. CRM systems enable businesses to manage and analyze customer interactions and data throughout the customer lifecycle. By centralizing customer information, businesses can track customer interactions, manage customer accounts, and deliver personalized service. This results in more effective communication, improved customer service, and opportunities for upselling and cross-selling.

Implementing AI and Machine Learning

Artificial Intelligence (AI) and machine learning are revolutionizing customer interactions. These technologies can analyze large volumes of data to predict customer preferences and behavior. For instance, AI-driven chatbots can provide instant customer support, handling inquiries and solving problems efficiently. Machine learning algorithms can also personalize marketing efforts, suggesting products or services that customers are more likely to be interested in, based on their past behavior.

Enhancing Customer Experiences with Augmented and Virtual Reality

Augmented Reality (AR) and Virtual Reality (VR) offer novel ways to engage customers. These technologies can create immersive and interactive experiences, whether it's for trying products virtually, experiencing services in a simulated environment, or providing engaging and interactive content. AR and VR can significantly enhance the customer experience, making interactions with your brand more memorable and impactful.

Optimizing with Data Analytics

Data analytics plays a crucial role in understanding customer interactions. By analyzing customer data, businesses can gain insights into customer preferences, behavior patterns, and satisfaction levels. This information can be used to tailor interactions, improve product offerings, and make informed decisions about marketing and sales strategies.

In the quest to enhance Customer Lifetime Value (CLV), businesses must embark on a multifaceted approach that encompasses understanding customers, improving product and service quality, personalizing experiences, fostering loyalty, maximizing engagement, and leveraging technology. Each of these strategies plays a critical role in building deeper, more meaningful relationships with customers. By prioritizing customer needs and preferences, continuously evolving with market demands, and embracing technological advancements, businesses can not only increase the value they derive from each customer but also establish a loyal customer base. Remember, the key to sustainable business growth lies in the value you provide to your customers and the experiences you create for them. In a world where customers have myriad choices, those businesses that focus on enhancing every aspect of the customer journey stand out and succeed in the long run.

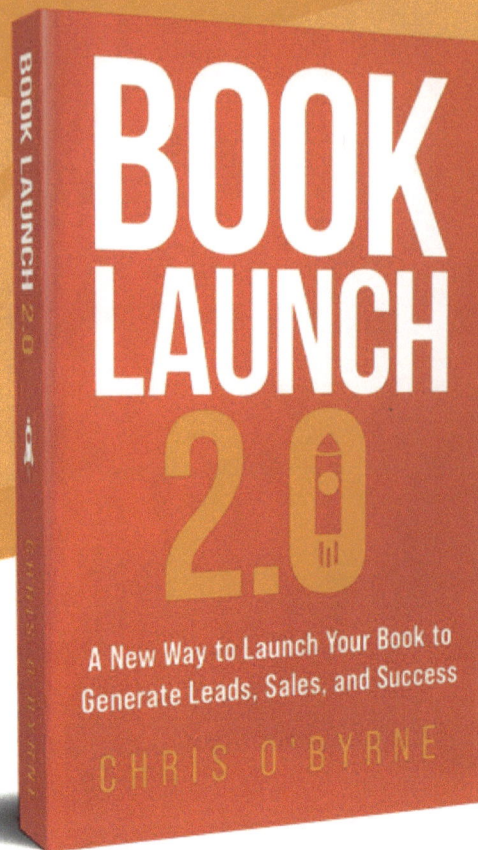